ONLINE TEACHING
AND
CLASSOROOM
MANAGEMENT

2 books in one: Zoom for Beginners

+

Google Classroom

2020
Amazon Books

Barbara Clark

Table of Content

ZOOM FOR BEGINNERS

A COMPLETE GUIDE TO TEACH ONLINE AND IMPROVE THE LEARNING OUTCOMES OF YOUR STUDENTS

INTRODUCTION TO ZOOM

Zoom is a pioneer (and possibly the packs most prominent since its April IPO) in the video correspondences industry, tending to computerized interchanges at all endpoints through their cloud stage for video, sound conferencing, coordinated effort, visiting, and online classes.

Zoom is a free service that lets you chat using big groups on a mobile device or personal computer. The difference between others, along with zoom chat solutions, is the variety of participants. A-Zoom assembly can, while Skype could get up to 50 callers in one meeting, have around a million participants, showing up in a grid design to 49 of these. Schools, businesses use meetings to be conducted by Zoom, maintain classes, and host virtual occasions. Another characteristic is that participants do not require perhaps or a Zoom accounts the Zoom program to combine a meeting. While this makes Zoom, bypassing those measures will restrict what you could do.

It is vital that before we research zoom any farther, zoom claims to possess encryption, meaning that Zoom ought to have the ability to get audio and assembly video. Zoom gets the capacity to get assembly data as they please, but studies have proven differently. This defect could compromise any information that is transmitted via the service. Zoom has information privacy issues. By way of instance, it's been captured sharing consumer information without the consumer's knowledge with firms like Facebook. Also, it keeps files, cloud records, and messages. For groups and businesses with vouchers, these subscriptions' administrators have a fantastic amount of power over their workers' accounts. They track their Zoom information or could combine any worker's assembly. The concern is known as zoo bombing. It is where users attempt to interrupt them by revealing offensive material. Zoom's founders added security upgrades, like requiring assembly passwords to fight such trolls. Because of these issues, several organizations have prohibited using Zoom. You can have an experience so long as you take precautions.

Zoom Overview

One gander at Zoom's site will disclose to you how well known the administration is. Zoom has tributes from the absolute most significant ventures on the planet, yet Zoom's not only for enormous name organizations, particularly following the pandemic of 2020, constraining everybody to telecommute. Zoom is currently utilized by little and enormous organizations the same, just as not-for-profits, governments, establishments, and people around the world, fulfilling an ever-developing need for keeping individuals associated.

What Are the Main Zoom Services?

Zoom's principle administration is video correspondences. The interface is straightforward enough for anybody to see how to utilize it in only a couple of moments. The application configuration includes a video "upfront" style approach with a solitary control bar on the base.

The Zoom meeting control bar highlights straightforward symbols that speak to the receiver control, camera use, members, talk, screen sharing, recording, and response. Zoom keeps up an oversimplified and natural interface, and a considerable lot of these symbols drill down to get to more profound degrees of control. In the engine, Zoom offers numerous video conferencing highlights that its rivals don't. Hence, Zoom has gotten the most loved for power clients who host loads of online gatherings. Clients frequently pick Zoom for its not insignificant rundown of highlights; however, the genuine excellence of Zoom is its dependability. Individuals love utilizing Zoom since its motivation constructed configuration works for them 99.99% of the time with no requirement for IT support. The effortlessness of the structure causes clients to feel like they are in charge of their gatherings.

HOW TO GET STARTED WITH ZOOM

Where to Download Zoom

After getting familiar with the zoom dashboard, the next practical step is to download the zoom to your computer to begin using it.

There are practically two ways of downloading zoom to your computer.

You Scroll down the page, under download, click on meetings client, and download.

OR

Go to host a meeting at the top right-hand corner of your dashboard,

Click on any of the options among the trio of with Video off, with Video on, or screen share only.

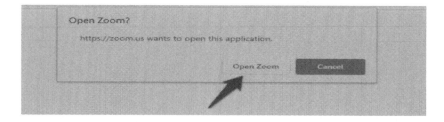

Zoom Subscription Plans

There are a few varieties worth referencing between the free Zoom and paid plans.

Free Users

The Zoom application can be introduced in your gadget or telephone, and you can go to any gathering with an ID given.

Paying Users

If your director framework has a Pro, Business, or Company account, you can download and join Zoom to your gadget through your work email. At that point, you need to synchronize Zoom with your schedule so you can mastermind Zoom gatherings and welcome far off members to take an interest. Zoom have various highlights for various record type and clients. All clients and record types have highlights custom fitted to their needs.

Sorts of records

There are four (4) sorts of Zoom accounts:

1. Basic or free record

2. Pro record

3. Business or Enterprise account

4. Education record

Zoom empowers one-on-one talk meetings that can transform into a gathering or group call, instructional meetings, and online classes for both inside and outside crowds, and global video gatherings and meetings with up to 1000 members and participants and up to 49 recordings on the presentation screen. The free arrangement permits boundless individual gatherings yet anyway restrains bunch meetings to 40 minutes and one hundred members.

Zoom gives four arrangement types (barring the Zoom Room membership):

1. Zoom essential or free arrangement

This arrangement is open and fundamental and permits clients to have a boundless number of individual gatherings and Group gatherings with 100 members and will break the following 40 minutes if three members join the gathering. This record doesn't bolster enormous gatherings, online classes, and meetings can't be recorded. It additionally empowers a boundless number of eyes to eye gatherings, video conferencing highlights, web conferencing highlights, and gathering cooperation highlights.

2. Zoom Pro arrangement

This arrangement costs $ 14.99/£ 11.99 every month per meeting and gathering host and $12.49 every year. It empowers hosts to make an individual gathering and meeting IDs for dreary Zoom gatherings, and it can record gatherings and gatherings in the cloud or your gadget. Empowers administrators to include orders, 1GB of cloud recording in MP4 or M4A position, client the board and use reports, and other discretionary extra highlights.

3. Zoom Business or endeavor plan

This arrangement costs $ 19.99/£ 15.99 every month per meeting, and gatherings have (10 least). It permits you to customize Zoom gatherings and gatherings with custom URLs and friends marking, and it gives records of Zoom gatherings and meetings recorded in the cloud, just as devoted client service. It additionally offers at least ten illustrators, devoted phone support, an executive dashboard, records of chronicles in the cloud. The yearly arrangement has even numerous highlights, for example, customized URL, marked improvement, and customized messages for business and undertakings and expenses $16.65 every year.

4. Zoom Education

Zoom training has boundless distributed storage for chronicles, perfect for organizations and associations with more than a thousand representatives. This arrangement costs $ 19.99/£ 15.99 every month per meeting, and gathering host (100 least) additionally has a customer achievement.

Creating Your Account

After downloading the app, the next task to perform is to perform a registration for the service. You can perform the task with your smartphone or personal computer, but we will firstly talk about the web service.

Navigate to the page for sign up, and you will find different options that you can utilize to create an account. The platform will demand a work email, but you should not worry about that because your email is enough and will function properly in the place of a work email.

The only risk attached to utilizing a personal email is that the app sometimes thinks that users with specific email domains work for the same organization. That is the privacy issues associated with the platform. However, you should know that the platform does not include some popular email domains such as Yahoo and Gmail in the generalization.

Users can also create a profile by selecting the login with Google or Facebook button on the login page, which will, in turn, download the program's application to your computer with just one click.

After inputting your email, the platform will send you an authorization email. Select the activate control key in the email to activate your account. You can also copy and paste the link to your browser to get your account activated.

When the page launches on your browser, input your names and passkey.

You can invite other attendants on the following page to create a free profile through email.

The platform will provide a link to the meeting URL for you, and you can select the begin meeting control key to start it. After performing that task, it will start downloading the app on your device. Let the quick guide you through the installation process.

After installing the app, there will be several buttons to help you navigate through the platform. You will find buttons like the sign in or attend a meeting. You can start a test meeting immediately by tapping login.

The following screen comes with text fields for your email and pass-key, the information required for you to log onto the platform.

After the login process, ensure that you are on your Home tab, then select the new meeting control key on your application, and it will start the meeting.

If you sign up for the platform through your mobile application, it has a related method of setting up and installing the web concept.

Get the Android or iOS app and launch it. It will display several options for you to navigate through different sections of the platform, which includes the sign in or sign up control keys to get started. Select sign up.

The following screen comes with text fields to input your names, email, and a box to check for the terms of services agreement. Select sign up, and the platform will send an authorization email for you to activate your account.

Select the activate control key provided in the email sent to you or copy and paste the URL included in the email into your browser.

The platform will ask you to finish the same steps required to create a profile through your browser.

After that, it will take you to the screen containing the begin meeting control key and your meeting URL. Feel free to select your desired choice, and it will take you to a waiting room for testing meetings.

You can start a meeting by clicking the sign-in control key below your visual display. Input your login details and select the sign-in control key on the following page. It will launch your text meeting in the application.

How to Access Zoom

After creating your account, it is straightforward to invite different participants to your meeting. The platform allows users to invite attendants to a meeting in various ways. If you utilize mobile or desktop applications, select the tab for meetings and follow the below instructions:

If you select the copy invitation control key while utilizing your desktop application, It will copy a message containing several important information. They include your meeting identity, URL, and mobile details to your clipboard, where you can drop a message or email.

Whenever you select the send invite control key on your mobile application, It will display three alternative options, send a message which lets users send a text the meeting URL to another person. Send an email for launching an email, including the details of your meeting and copy to the clipboard. It copies information like the identity and URL of your meeting to your mobile's clipboard.

Users also have the option of inviting several other participants while in use:

If you utilize a desktop application, navigate to your toolbar by moving the mouse inside the window for your meetings and select the invite control key. After performing that task, the platform will launch a window for you to invite your contacts, send information through email on how to participate in the meeting. Then copy the URL of your meeting to your clipboard.

If you utilize a mobile application, select participants, and click on the invite control key beneath your following visual display. After performing that task, the platform will let you send an invitation through email, text messages, and perform several other tasks.

Upgrade Your Zoom Account

Here, we will be talking about how to upgrade your account to the desired plan. I know by now you must have gotten yourself acquainted with a particular plan, and you are perplexed as regards upgrading it. With the simple instructions I will be given here, you will realize that it is not hard as you must have anticipated.

Now let's roll into getting your account upgraded for you

Click on the top right of your Zoom application

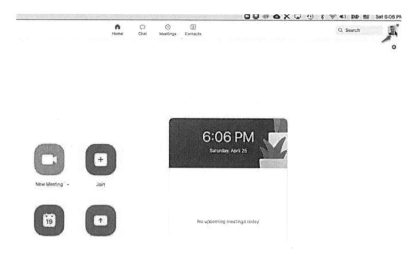

Here several options will pop up, just click on buy license

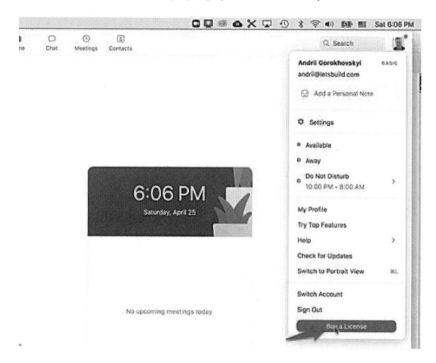

Here you will be directed to your profile; all you have to do is click on plans and pricing

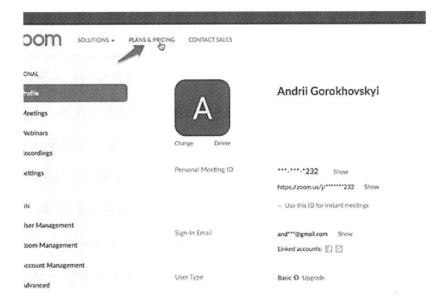

Then select the plan you want to buy

Select the plan if it will be annually or monthly and click on continue below the image

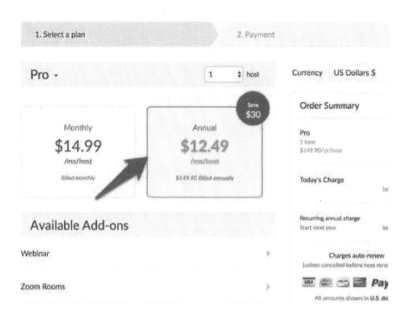

You will be asked for other details; just input them

After you must have fill in your details, type in the details asked regarding your credit card and then clicked on upgrade

Payment Method

Andrii Gorokhovskyi

Credit Card Num

CVV

Expirat

2021

Full Address   Same as Bill To Contact

I'm not a robot

reCAPTCHA

I agree to the Privacy Policy and Terms of Service

Back

Upgrade Now

Zoom Video Conferencing

How to Start A New Meeting on Zoom?

If you are hosting a meeting, click on the 'New Meeting' option represented by the orange icon. You will enter an interface that enables you to change the settings according to your preferences.

Share Screen Toolbars

These are the tools used in carrying out some tasks in the shared screen feature

Let's quickly discuss the toolbars above

Unmute/ Mute: This allows you to mute your microphone so that the participants can hear you and also unmute your microphone if you want them to hear from you.

Start video: With this, the host can decide to stop or start the video

Manage Participants: This allows you to manage participants such as mute/unmute microphones, start/stop the camera, lock screen, share, lock the meeting, etc.

New Share: This allows you to go back to the screen selection window to share a different window and restart a window that has been shared before.

Pause/Share: This allows you to pause a window being shared and also to continue it after being paused

Annotate: This is used to make online drawing, text insertion within the screen sharing in the Zoom window. It is also used to point out important information with a spotlight tool.

More: This tool opens a drop-down menu that contains additional menu items like chat, breakout room, invite, record to the cloud, disable attendee annotation

Now let's talk on how to share screen on a Zoom application.

How to Share Screen and A Portion of a Screen?

Let's assume you host a meeting you intend sharing a file that requires you to share the screen; this is how to go about it

Click on the share screen button below the screen

Here in this place, some windows will pop up showing you what you can share, click on what you intend sharing

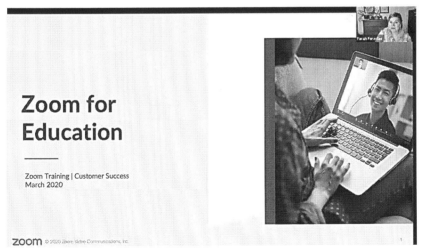

What you click will be seen in this page

Let's assume there is a part of a work done you are not willing to disclose to your participants; there is a feature in sharing screen that permits that, and it is called "Portion of a screen."

Now let's talk about how to share a portion of a screen

Open the file you wish to share a portion of in the background

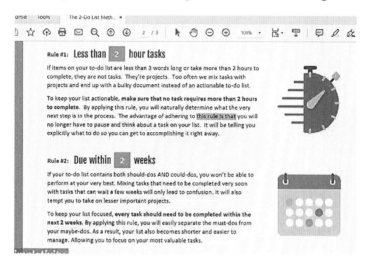

Go back to the share screen and click on advanced

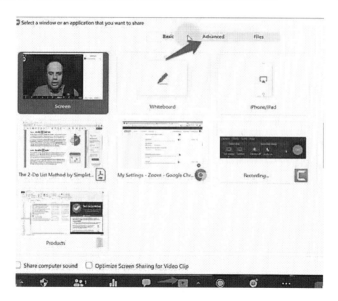

When the screen pops up, click on the portion of the screen and also on the share button

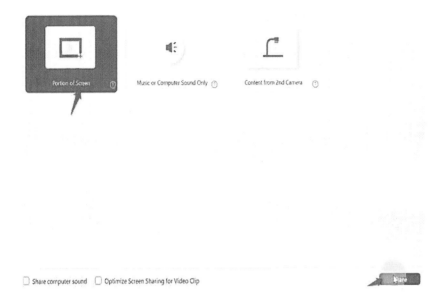

By selecting share, you automatically go back the file you wish to share a portion with a green rectangular shape around it

Note: The section covered with the rectangular shape is the only part available for the participants to see. However, the rectangular shape can be dragged

around to show any other part the host wishes to share, and when this happens, the color around the file changes to yellow.

How to Stop Participants from Sharing Screen?

Click on settings when you open your Zoom app

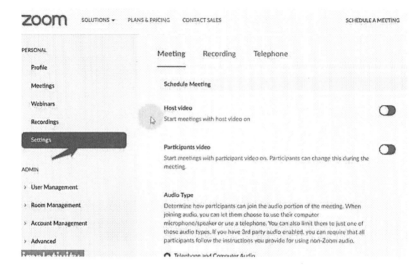

Scroll down until you get to screen sharing then click on the only host can share

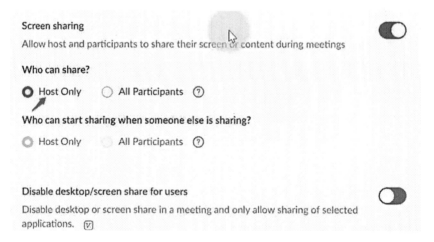

How to Share Video on Zoom?

If you want to share a video with your participants, follow the steps below

Click on the share screen button below the screen

Here in this place, some windows will pop up showing you what you can share; click on the video you intend sharing

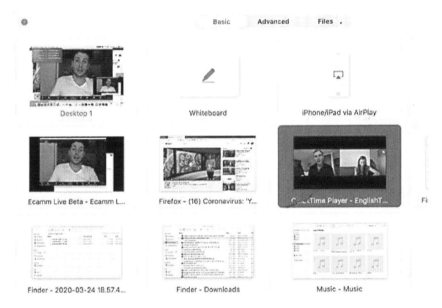

Below the screen, click on share sound so that the participants can hear the sound of the video and optimize screen share for a video clip to make the video quality high

Click on share below the right-hand side of the screen

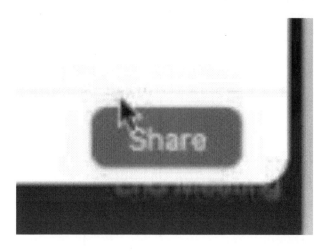

Here on this page, the video shared will be seen by the participants

ZOOM TIPS AND TRICKS PART ONE

Quick Invitation

Whenever you are in an interaction, and you remembered that you didn't invite a particular person related to the topic of discussion. You can solve that problem quickly wit this attribute. Launch the invite page and select email, copy the address, and transfer it to the person to invite them into the conversation. You can perform this task with your workers as well as friends and family.

Automatically Scheduled Meetings, Notification of Participants

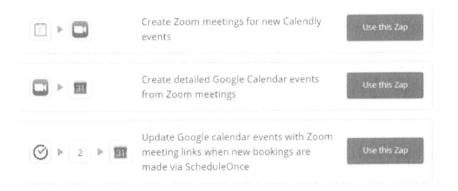

If you run a lot of meetings--for example, with customers Do not have an assistant, you may want to join Zoom, your scheduling program, and your calendar. Whenever someone at a scheduling program books a scheduled appointment, Zapier can produce a new Zoom assembly and insert it. With all those programs you use, below are a few Zaps to electricity this particular workflow.

However, you can produce a Zap. You can add a to make this automation a more decisive measure that shares the assembly details and your group using a program like Slack. This automation is used all of the time by us at Zapier; the Zoom connection has been posted to the station in Slack.

Create Recurring Appointments with Saved Settings and One URL

This feature works well when you need to host a similar topic with a set crowd at regular intervals, like a yoga teacher giving classes, or a spiritual leader providing virtual space for their congregation.

When a meeting is set as Recurring, all the settings you specify for it will remain unchanged, including the link, passcode, and Meeting ID. For this reason, it is recommended that you never use your Personal Meeting ID for Recurring meetings, as the value and utility of your PMID are that it is constant even for Instant meetings. This value gets lost if you reserve it according to a strict recurring schedule when an automatically generated ID would've fulfilled the same role in this case.

Anyway, once the rest of your meeting settings are finalized, select the calendar you wish to add to (or just select "Add to Calendar" if applicable), then select "Schedule." It is highly recommended that you schedule using Google Calendar.

When doing so, you'll then be prompted by Google to sign in and select your Google Account if you haven't already, and may be asked to let Zoom access your Google account. Allow Zoom to do so. You will then be shown options for how your meeting should recur; daily, weekly on the day you set (e.g., every Wednesday if your meeting will first commence on a Wednesday), monthly, annually, every weekday, or some other custom arrangement.

When you're happy with the way your scheduled meeting will recur, select "Save."

You can also use Outlook as your calendar if your Zoom app is on a mobile device, where the process is highly similar. You can technically use Outlook on Windows and Mac too, but it is not recommended; Google Calendar is far simpler and easier to use in this case, especially if you're also using Calendly.

Verification of Those Who Present

When making use of zoom, it is sometimes impossible to meeting members to see the person who is hosting the meeting. It is essential to see the person who is talking as the body language of the person may provide more clues into understanding the subject matter. Imagine a scenario in which meeting members introduce themselves by saying their names before sharing a thought o asking a question. Until people in a meeting becomes familiar with the person heading a meeting, there is a certain level of communication that may not be achieved.

Mute Audio

It is one of the most exciting attributes of the platform. It gives users the power to minimize and eradicate background noise and cross-talks, especially when there are many attendants on the video interaction. You can perform this task with a simple click.

For instance, if you find yourself in a conference on the web and have nothing to contribute at that moment, you can quickly mute your mic, and whenever you want to contribute, you can turn it back for usage. You can turn it on by holding your space bar, which will turn on the mic, and you can start talking. If you take your hands off the space bar, the mic goes mute again.

The feature ensures that you have a smooth interaction without interruptions and do not take lots of bandwidth. It also offers excellent clarity of voice, which means that everyone can hear each other. If you want to utilize this attribute, launch settings, select audio, allow mute mic anytime you want to join an interaction. It makes the whole process easy and straightforward.

Mute Everyone

You can mute all your participants after admitting them from the Waiting room. Participants still have the opportunity to unmute themselves, so you have to put a permanent control over the mute setting from your end as the host which the participants can be able to unmute.

Click the Manage Participants menu, locate the Mute all button, and click on it.

Uncheck the Allow participants unmute themselves box, then click on the Continue button.

With this setting, your participants won't be able to unmute themselves throughout the session of your meeting.

Disable Video

The disallow feature can save you from that embarrassment. There is an option for you to disallow the feature permanently anytime you want to link up with an interaction. Whenever you're fit enough to face the camera, you can turn it back on and use it. If you want to utilize this attribute, navigate to your settings, and launch it, select the video and allow turn my video off anytime, you join a meeting.

Record the Call as A Video

Zoom enables you to capture calls. You need permission to do so. The meeting host might need to allow records. It is well worth checking your account settings to be sure before you begin recording is enabled.

- Log in to your Zoom accounts

- Click to see Account Settings/Meeting configurations

- Navigate into the Recording tab and then click on to allow video recording

It is worth noting that the recording can be activated by Zoom admins for everybody, for groups of consumers. There is advice on preferences. To document a Zoom assembly, you have to choose whether to utilize the cloud or local alternative. Local means you save the video file yourself in a different storage area or on your personal computer. Using Cloud, which will be for subscribers, Zoom shops the video for you. However, to capture videos, you will need to zoom on macOS, Windows, or even Linux. After you capture a meeting and select Record into the Cloud, the video, music, and chat are listed from the Zoom cloud.

Whenever the Zoom call starts, you ought to see a Choice On the base of the screen. Clicking that enables you to record at or locally the cloud. If you do not find the choice to record, assess your preferences from the web app (beneath My Meeting Settings) or have the admin of your account empower it. The files streamed from a browser or may be downloaded into a pc. Throughout the interview, you might even see which participants are recording the meeting, and also, those around the assembly will be informed while the assembly is being listed. After the phone is finished, Zoom will convert the recording into an MP4 video document that is usable.

ZOOM TIPS AND TRICKS PART TWO

Conduct Joint Annotation

Display sharing enables a telephone to display host whatever to everybody on the telephone on their display. Annotation tools allow the assembly participants to emphasize what and draw useful when talking materials, like mockups, graphic designs, etc. To annotate while seeing the shared display of someone else, Select View Choice choose Annotate. A Toolbar appears with your choices draw on, such as text, arrow, and so on. The presenter may use the button on the toolbar to capture the whole image. You can also disable attendee annotation.

Combined Calls

There are methods by inputting to combine a Zoom assembly—a Meeting ID, together with your internet browser, or clicking on an invitation connection.

- To combine with the Meeting ID:

- In the Zoom main display, click on Join.

- Enter the Meeting ID and click on Join.

- Input the password, and then click Join Meeting.

- You will be asked if you would like to connect with or without a video. Select Join with Video.

32

- Before you go into space, you might be put from the Waiting Room first. Until the server permits you to combine, if that's the case, you're remaining here.

To combine with an Invitation connection:

A different means is via an invitation connection. Zoom will inquire if you would like the program to shoot over when you click on a Zoom connection. Select available Zoom, and you're going to go through the procedure of connecting the assembly. You might have to give Zoom consent to use the microphone and your camera, especially when this is the very first meeting.

Record the Meeting in The Cloud

Approved clients of Pro, Business, and Enterprise records can record their gatherings and store them in the cloud. Zoom likewise gives a wide range of recording formats, such as Active Speaker, Gallery View, or Screen Share, permitting you to pick the design that best suits your present needs.

Be that as it may, distributed storage is restricted to 1GB or 0.5GB for most membership designs just, and you have to make an extra buy if you need more extra room. The cloud enrollment choice might be impaired as a matter of course, so on the off chance that you need to empower it in your record, in a gathering you have made, or for end clients, you should follow the means underneath.

Sign in to your record as a chairman who has the authorization to change account settings and snap the Account Management alternative in the route sheet. Go to account settings, open the enrollment tab, and actuate cloud enlistment. Alternatively, you can disable the cloud log download choice if you don't need anybody to download your recordings.

You should tap the User Management menu and afterward select the Group Management alternative. Discover the gathering you need to empower this choice, click on it, and afterward click on the Settings button. Go to the Recording tab and enact the cloud recording capacity.

End clients can initiate cloud enlistment by tapping the Settings button in the route sheet and opening the Registration tab. Enact the cloud enlistment choice and affirm the progressions you made.

Zoom permits you to alter Cloud Recording settings once the choice is empowered so you can pick the account design, or if you need to record sound just or spare talk messages from the gathering. Also, you can consequently decipher sound chronicles, add timestamps to video accounts, or decide to show the names of the chronicle members.

At the point when you're prepared, you should begin another gathering, however, know that lone has and has can begin another cloud sign-in meeting. Snap the Register fasten and pick the cloud enrollment choice starting from the drop menu.

You can tap the "Stop," or "Delay" catches on the off chance that you need to quit recording a gathering whenever, while recording will naturally stop after the Zoom meeting closes. Zoom will begin preparing the video when the account meeting closes; the application will send you an email warning once the video is accessible.

Delegation of Duties

There are a few jobs accessible for a gathering: We have the host, co-have, elective host, and members. The host chooses the job that you have in a gathering.

Host

The client plans the gathering. They have the full position to deal with the gathering. Just one host exists in a gathering

Co-Host

Has the more significant part of the host's controls, empowering the co-host to deal with the regulatory territories of the gathering? The host must allot a co-have during the gathering. The co-have can't begin a gathering. Maybe the host needs another person to begin the gathering, and an elective host can be allocated.

Elective hosts

Offers indistinguishable consents from the co-have, however, can go a beginning further to begin a gathering. An elective host can be chosen when a gathering is being planned.

Host and co-have controls in a gathering

Different parts of a zoom meeting, such as dealing with the members, can be constrained by the host.

Facilitating benefits can be shared by different clients to deal with the authoritative side of the gathering through the co-have highlight. A co-have must be allotted by the host, as there is no confinement on the quantity of co-has you can have in a Meeting or Webinar.

Inspect Your Appearance

This additional beauty filter is useful when you are just out of bed and need to attend an important meeting. It provides a dewy and filtered touch-up to your face, offering a fresh look. At times, video calls can alter your look despite dressing up and wearing makeup. It is when the beauty feature can come in handy. It makes you look well-rested by smoothing your facial features.

To access this feature, tap the up arrow next to the Start Video button and click on Video Settings. You will find 'Touch Up My Appearance' below My Video. Check the box, and you are ready to go.

Use Some Important Keyboard Shortcuts

Console alternate ways are amazingly helpful on the off chance you despise floating over the screen with a mouse. Essential capacities, for example, sharing your screen, recording your screen, changing to a full screen see, and joining a gathering can be accomplished with alternate console routes.

Here are the real console alternate routes for daily activities (given a MacBook console format):

Meeting Shortcuts

- Command (⌘) +J: Join Meeting

- Command (⌘) +Control + V: Start Meeting

- Command (⌘) +J: Schedule Meeting

- Command (⌘) +Control + S: Screen Share using Direct Share

- Command (⌘) +Shift + A: Mute/unmute sound

- Command (⌘) +Control + M: Mute sound for everybody aside from the host (just accessible to the host)

- Command (⌘) +Shift + C: Start cloud recording

- Command (⌘) +Shift + P: Pause or resume recording

Visit Shortcuts

- CTRL: Switch starting with one tab then onto the next

- In any case, there are certain requirements to utilize these easy console routes, which are:

- Windows Desktop Client Version 3.5.19869.0701 or higher

- Mac Desktop Client Version 3.5.19877.0701 or higher

- Linux Desktop Client Version 1.1.32904.1120 or higher

- iPad with iOS App Version 4.4.5 (55341.0715) or higher

You can likewise alter the easy console routes dependent on your inclination by going to Settings and afterward, Accessibility. Snap-on the alternate route and press the easy route key to alter it.

Transfer Files in Chat During Zoom Conference

If you have a file you like to share with your participants using the in-meeting chat, click on the Chat menu, and use the option to select who should have access to the file. If you want the file to be sent to everyone in the meeting, leave it as it is.

Select your file and upload it.

If sent to everyone, only participants actively in the meeting will have access to download the file.

ZOOM FOR TEACHERS

Zoom Online Teaching - How to Use Zoom to Teach

Teaching Online Lessons with Zoom

As a course instructor, all you will need is a zoom account. You do need a microphone and a webcam if not built into whatever device you are using. A headset microphone recommends for better sound quality. Using the web-based zoom application gives you a better experience as a course instructor.

Login to zoom.us to start.

Scheduling a lesson and settings

Once you are okay with your account registration, go to my account and then schedule a meeting immediately. It is where you can customize your session or lesson.

If you are using the free version of zoom, you will have a limit of 40 minutes with three participants. To have more time you, may have to Upgrade, or the other option starts the lesson multiple times.

Start by entering the information for your meeting.

For security reasons, do well to add a password to your meetings.

Turn on Video for Host and off for participants. It will allow only you, the Host, to share your screen or camera once the meeting starts. Students can't share their screen or camera with Video turn off in the settings. It is a security feature to have to prevent zoom bombers from sharing irrelevant things.

To prevent your students from joining the meeting with background noise, you may need to mute participants upon entry.

Another setting to keep your meetings safe from zoom bombers requires enabling a waiting room. Your students will have to wait in the waiting room until they get admitted by you, the Host, to the central meeting.

Click on the Save button when done.

Sending invitation to students

As the Host, you will need to share your meeting link with your students to join the meeting.

Copy and share the invitation link with your students through their email or a learning management system. Your students should follow other meeting from their computer or any mobile device as well. Students will need to use the App Zoom to have access to the forum.

Starting your online lessons

To Begin your online lecture as the instructor, click on the Start this Meeting button on the zoom web. Your meeting will automatically begin. If a message pops up without the start of the session, click on the Open Zoom meetings. On your computer, the client-based zoom app will automatically turn on, so at this time, you allow it to complete the setup process.

Below the zoom window, you have the microphone and video icons. Select the video or microphone icon to transform it off or on. Only turn on your Video if you want your students to see you. Ensure your background looks professional and dressed adequately before turning on Video.

When your students begin to join your lesson, notify through the Manage Participants menu. Click on the Manage participants menu to see your students in the waiting room.

Before you go ahead to admit your students into the meeting room, click on the More or 3-dots Button to carry out the following settings below the waiting room.

Ensure that the participants to unmute themselves and allow participants to rename themselves are not enabled.

When you click on the Mute Participants upon Entry option, ensure you don't enable the Allow participants to unmute themselves. Only click on the continue button to complete the mute setting. It will give you the Host, complete control over your student's microphone usage.

When done with the settings, you can start admitting students into the meeting room.

To take your students' questions during a lesson, you can manually unmute the particular student you want to listen to by going to the participant panel.

The Chat menu on the zoom window allows you to send text messages to your students.

You can chat with a particular student or the entire student in your meeting room.

You can also use the chat panel to share files with your students.

Only participants present will have access to the file when done uploading it.

To prevent your students from chatting with each other during a lesson using Zoom, click on the 3-dots and select the option participants can chat with Host Only.

Tips and Tricks for Virtual Lessons

• For your first class, set aside some time to introduce your students to Zoom and ensure that they're able to connect their audio and video.

• Give an agenda or plan for each class by Screen Sharing a document or slide at the beginning of class. This gives students a clear idea of how the class will progress, what will be covered, and the activities they'll engage in.

• Discuss online etiquette and expectation of the students in your first virtual class and periodically revisit the topics.

• Utilize the Whiteboard or Annotate a shared document and let your students engage as well. When sharing a whiteboard, document, screen, or image, try whiteboarding math problems or have a student use annotation to highlight items such as grammar mistakes in a paper you're sharing.

• Take time to promote questions, comments, and reactions from your class. Give a minute to allow your students to utilize reactions, write their questions in chat, or be unmuted to ask their questions live.

• Divide into smaller groups for a discussion on a specific topic. You can use Zoom's Breakout Room feature to either pre-assign or auto-assign students into groups for a short period so they may discuss things together.

• Have students be the presenter and share projects with the class. This allows your students to show what they're working while practicing their presentation skills. It also allows students to hear from one another.

Tips for Running Large Meeting Sessions

1.   Have a co-presenter to help facilitate the Zoom session with you; especially if you are allowing chat messages and in case you have any unexpected issues.

2.   Ensure your session is well planned and it has opportunities for the attendees to engage to keep their attention actively.

3.   Add your noted and changes to this checklist, such as 'what went well' and 'what could be improved in the future.'

What Can Students Do in Zoom?

Besides just voice-chatting, zoom gives students plenty of tools to interact with each other and the teacher, work together, and even break off into smaller groups just as if they were sitting with each other in a classroom. But if teachers don't need these capabilities for class, or if they're causing problems, they can all be turned off. With a little preparation, setting some norms and frontloading critical digital citizenship skills, you and your students can enjoy the benefits of Zoom's interactive features. Here's just a sampling of what you can do if these features are enabled:

1. Share Screen: This allows the entire class to view one person's computer screen. Students can even annotate a document on another student's computer. Teachers can restrict this so only the teacher's screen can be shared. Teachers can also disable the annotation feature so students can't annotate.

2. Whiteboard: This is a brainstorming tool that let students toss ideas around, such as for a group project.

3. Breakout Rooms: The teacher can divide students up into smaller groups, then bring the entire class back together. Teachers can pre-assign the groups before class, assign them manually during the meeting, or have Zoom randomly break students into groups.

4. Raise Hand, Clap, Disagree, Speed Up, Slow Down: These are icons students can use to let the teacher know they have a question or comment, react to something, or ask the teacher to talk faster or slower.

5. Chat with the Group: Students can send a message to the entire class.

6. Private Chat: Just like passing noted, students can send direct, personal messages to other kids in the class. The teacher can't view private chats between students. The teacher can disable this feature for students.

Useful Teaching Features

Some in-office departments will not be able to deal with video conferencing and the potential difficulties that it presents. To make you more comfortable, here are some tips to help group members to conduct Zoom conferences and call seamlessly. Set aside some room for your first lesson to expose the students to the Zoom and make sure their audio and video connections.

• Have an objective or schedule by Screen Sharing a paper or slide at the beginning of the course for each lesson. It adds up to students have a clear idea of how the class will proceed, what is going to be covered, and the tasks they are going to engage in.

• Explore web behavior and student standards in the first simulated lesson, then refresh the topics daily.

• Use a shared document in the Whiteboard or transcribe it, and let your learners also engage.

• Where to share a Whiteboard, paper, screen, or photograph, seek math problems with whiteboarding, or let participants use annotation.

- Identify items like grammar errors in a paper you share.

- Taking the opportunity to progress the class questions, feedback, and responses. Give your users a minute to let them using answers, write in conversation, or be unmuted to ask any questions live.

- Divide the conversation into smaller units on a given topic. You may use the Breakout Room feature in Zoom on pre-assign students to attend classes for a limited period so that they can

- Being the presenter, share the initiatives with the class. It helps the students to demonstrate what you are presenting.

- Focus on student's delivery skills as they work. It also encourages learners to hear from each other.

- Pre-arrange the meeting and silence the microphones of the member upon entry. It helps to prevent background noise and allows for your students will focus on the class.

- Aim at the monitor and get the students into eye touch. It tends to establish a more intimate link throughout teaching.

- Take a second to test conversation or video of your students to check-in and receive input from the teachers.

- Talk as though you are connected explicitly to the class while making sure you are at the proper distance to the microphone for excellent hearing performance.

- Sharing photos, files, or videos while giving a presentation offer the students a chance to loosen up or breathe in what you have shared.

- Take a break after you stop debate and encourage the students to participate before moving further.

THE MOST COMMON ZOOM PROBLEMS AND HOW TO FIX THEM

Telecommuting is on the rise today, and more companies are turning to video conferencing to keep their employees informed. But nothing is more uncomfortable than leading a meeting and seeing some flaws emerge. Some of us also use Zoom for personal calls, but no matter what the purpose is, we don't like to get in trouble, either. We've collected the most common problems Zoom users face and present step-by-step ways to fix them.

Webcam or Audio Not Working

Not working Nothing is more frustrating than not having your webcam or audio running on a Zoom call. If your webcam is missing or selected and not working in Zoom, you can try some of these basic tips first. When you join a call, Zoom presents the option to join the video before joining the meeting. Always click this button, or you will enter the call without the signal from the camera. If your webcam does not appear, the first thing to do is verify that all other software applications using the webcam are shut down. Zoom won't be able to use a camera if you have already granted it access in a different app. If your audio is still not working, you can test your audio and video in Zoom by clicking this link. Once open, you can enter the call usually in the Zoom app and follow the instructions on the screen if you are logged into the web (or just to double-check your webcam in the main Zoom app, (it can be Stop Video if you are on a call). The screen is blank, and you can click the arrow next to the video camera icon and choose the Same as a system or webcam with a more specific name from the list.

Sometimes, however, the problem may not be the zoom. If you are on a Windows 10 or a macOS device, the webcam may be blocked. You can fix this by checking the app permissions to make sure the Zoom app or web browser can use your webcam. Specifically, on the web, you can also verify these settings by restarting your call and making sure to hit Allow when asked about access to the camera and microphone.

In Windows, you can check if your webcam is blocked by searching for Webcam in the Start menu and selecting select which apps can use a camera from the dashboard. Scroll down, and you will see the list of applications that can use your webcam. Make sure your web browser or the Zoom box is checked. Similarly, you can also search for Microphone and choose microphone privacy settings to do the same.

On macOS, click to check the Security & Privacy in System Settings, click the lock, and enter your password to make changes. Then you can click on Camera in the sidebar and make sure the web browser and Zoom are selected. You should also check that the microphone box is also checked.

Echoes During A Call

Another common problem with Zoom is an audio echo during a meeting. If you hear echo or audio comments during the meeting, there are three possible reasons. First, someone could have the audio from the computer and the phone active at the same time. In that case, you'll want to ask them to leave one for the other manually. They will have to hang up or leave the audio on during the session by clicking the microphone icon and opt for Exit Computer Audio.

One other reason may be that people with computers or speakerphones are very close to each other. Lastly, multiple computers with active audio can be in the same conference room. To solve any of these other situations, you will have to ask the two people who are very close to you to move away. Or ask one of them to exit the conference call or mute the audio on the device.

Problems with Zoom Lagging or Freezing During Meetings

Delays and crashes often indicate a problem with your Internet connection. If you are using a mobile device, try going to an area with a more stable internet to see if that helps. You should also look for the proper internet speeds for a successful video chat. In a team environment, when talking to multiple people, you'll want to achieve a download speed of around 1 Mbps and an upload speed of 800 kbps. You can always check your current speeds with a quick internet speed test.

You can improve the video quality by changing the zoom setting as well. For example, disabling the HD options or the "Touch up my appearance" setting will decrease the amount of bandwidth required by your video connection (and the overhead on your system hardware) and can help correct lag issues.

Problems Sharing a Screen

If you are to share your screen during a call, you may need to check some settings first. Be sure of a stable internet connection and are connected to the call. Sharing your screen takes a lot of bandwidth. It's also a good idea to test a screen share meeting in Zoom first. You can do this by selecting Start without video on the Home tab when starting or joining a meeting. Your meeting will start with just audio conferences, freeing up some bandwidth. Your video will not connect automatically. Alternatively, if you're already on a call and need to share your screen, try turning off the video by clicking the Stop Video button and then choosing the green Share Screen button.

Problems with a Remote Control While Screen Sharing

When sharing your screen, the person looking at your screen can request the remote control to help solve the problem or explain a process more clearly in Options is a tool to request the remote control at any time while sharing.

If you want to start the remote control, but it is not working correctly, there are several possible problems to consider:

1. Sharing is not accepting the request: a notification will appear on your screen, and you will have to choose Allow screen sharing.

2. Sharing is interrupting the process: Technically, the person sharing your screen can stop the remote control at any time by

clicking the mouse. Occasionally, people are always doing something that ends the remote-control session before you can do anything. Always remind people to leave their computers alone while you take the remote control.

3. You may be on the wrong device - iPad and Android devices, for example, currently don't allow remote control request or provision.

Problems Receiving Email Messages from Zoom

Another common problem is that you cannot receive email messages from Zoom. This may include activation emails and notifications. They usually take 30 minutes to arrive and may take longer, but if not, make sure your email is set up correctly.

Problems with Zoom Crashing

If the zoom locks and closes completely, your first step should be to check the status of the zoom service and drop detector to see if there is a regional zoom problem in your area. Sometimes, problems with the servers or Zoom are doing maintenance on the platform, which simply means that the service will be down for a while, and you will have to wait for it to work again.

Try the web version of Zoom instead of the app if it doesn't look regional as long as the internet connection is stable, the web version tends to be a bit more reliable if the app has issues. Finally, take a look at your peripheral's settings. Sometimes zooming can get very confusing about video and audio settings. If you're trying to use your webcam connection as an audio output, for example, it often starts to hang. Make sure the video connections are directed to your webcam and, if necessary, the audio is directed to the associated speakers.

ZOOM BOMBING

What Is Zoom Bombing?

This is the cyber-attack that happens during the Zoom meeting, where an individual or group of individuals barge into a meeting without the permission of the host. Most times, when this happens, the intruders share offensive or explicit images or hate speech.

In this period of the pandemic, zoom bombing has become so rampant that several allegations have been held against Zoom—Inc. in their attempt of not being able to control the situation up to expectations.

How to Stop Zoom Bombing During A Meeting

Meeting Password

This is activated while scheduling a meeting. Only the invited participants can join the meetings; thus, disallowing intruders can come in between the meeting.

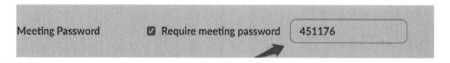

Allowing Only the Host to Share Screen

Another way to stop Zoom bombing is to allow only the host can share screen.

Click on settings when you open your Zoom app

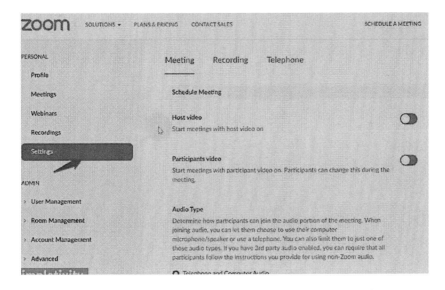

Scroll down until you get to screen sharing then click on the only host can share

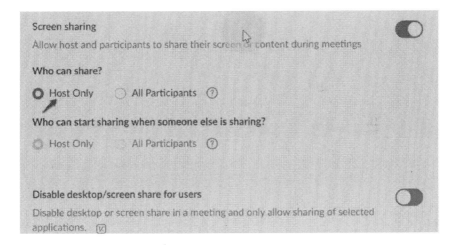

The Waiting Room

The easiest way to eliminate intruders is in the waiting room. With the waiting room, attendees cannot join the meeting until the host individually permits them from the waiting room. If the waiting room feature is enabled, the option for the invitees to join the meeting is disabled until the host arrives.

In the waiting room, the host can check if there is an intruder among the invitees, and if there is, he removes the intruder.

Let's quickly talk about how to enable the waiting room

When you open your Zoom application, go to your settings

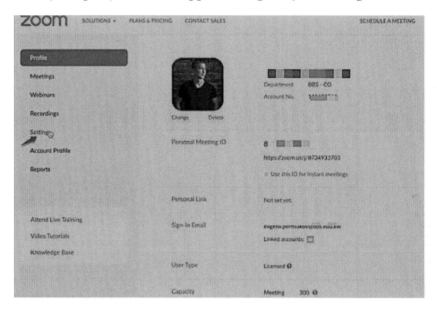

Move to the hand right side and scroll down to the waiting room and turn on the waiting room

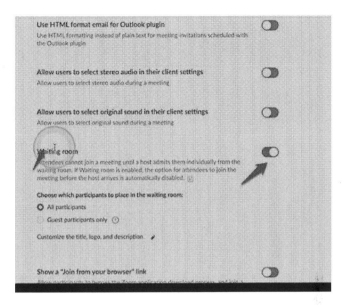

When the meeting commences, the host can see the invitees at the right-hand side before he admits or remove them

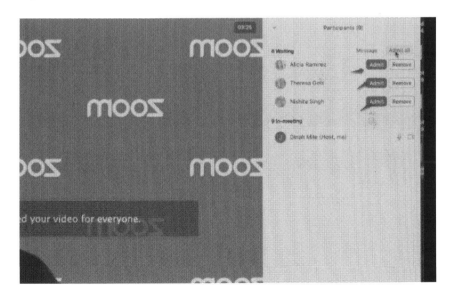

Lock Meeting Features

This feature also helps stop intruders from entering into a zoom meeting. With this feature, the host can lock the group when the participants have joined the meetings.

With the following steps, you can lock a meeting

Once the meeting has commenced, click on manage participants

The participants available will be shown on the right-hand side of the screen, then click on more

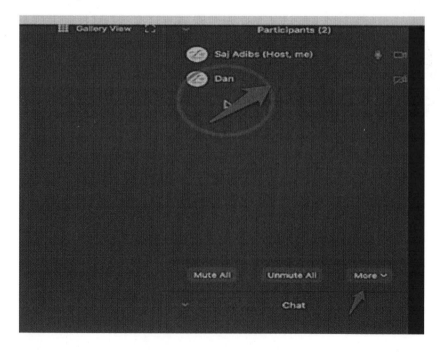

On this page, several options will come up, then click on lock meeting

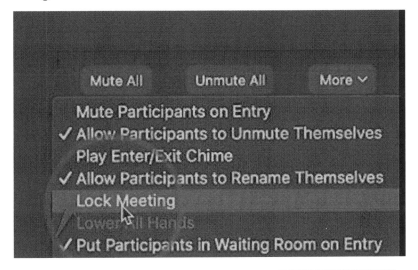

On the screen, there will be a pop up that says no attendee can join the meeting when it is locked, then click on ok. With this, the screen is locked.

PRIVACY AND SECURITY

How Can I Maximize the Security of My Zoom Classes?

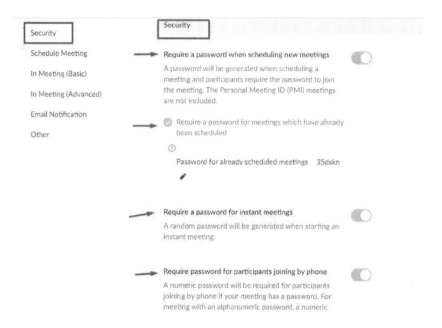

Before you continue utilizing the platform for your business and other purposes, you must understand the privacy and security issues of the platform.

The platform claims to utilize the end-to-end concept of encryption, and that means that it should not have access to video and audio communications. However, the reverse is the case, and the platform can access, host a video meeting, interaction, and serve several other purposes at any given time and location. It is a flaw that can jeopardize important information distributed through the platform.

There have been lots of reports about data privacy issues associated with the platform. You should also know that organizations with paid accounts have lots of control over their workers. They can join any meeting hosted by any worker and also keep track of their data without permission or knowledge.

Lastly, another primary concern is zoom-bombing. It is the location where users get access to meetings and try to interfere by displaying forbidden materials in the meeting. The producers of the platform found a method of combating that problem by ensuring that each user meets the password requirements by default.

Zoom Security Tips

Like practically everything else online, zoom meetings are also susceptible to uninvited intrusions and even mischief from invitees. Luckily, Zoom has come up with ways of securing your meetings against gate crashers, a phenomenon called Zoom bombing. Some of the security tips are listed below.

• As a rule of thumb, when you share your meeting link on social media or other public forums, that makes your event too public, as anyone with the link can join in on your meeting, even if the person wasn't expressly invited. Keep your meeting links within your circles.

• Zoom advises its users to avoid using their Meeting ID (PMI) to host public events. There's the option to generate random meeting IDs that one can use to host public events. The reason is simple, seeing as your PMI doesn't change unless you change it, using it to host public events only broadens the scale of uninvited people who can Zoom bomb you, and that could be very annoying as you can imagine. Your PMI should only be used to host meetings between you and other personal contacts you allow to contact you.

• Zoom recommends that you familiarize yourself with its settings and features to fully understand how to protect your virtual space on the fly from crashes and mischief-makers. Some of these features include the following;

i. Waiting Room: It's one of the best ways to protect your Zoom virtual events and keep out those who shouldn't be there. It allows you to send all participants to a virtual waiting area from where you can vet and admit them individually into the event. It also allows you to send only guest participants to the waiting area, in which case, frequent participants can proceed directly to the event without going through the waiting area.

ii. Locking the event: Once all your attendees have arrived, you can easily lock your meeting from the security menu, preventing additional attendees from joining.

iii. You also can turn off in-meeting features like chats and annotations. While these are great for collaboration, they are also easily used for mischief and distracting the meetings.

iv. Many more security and privacy tips are available on the Zoom website.

What Are the Safest Settings for Zoom Meetings?

Having clarified the problems that Zoom has had, let's see how you can prevent future problems so that your security is not affected.

While it is true that there is no manual to make a meeting by Zoom 100% safe, you can indeed take a series of precautionary measures so that it does not happen.

The first 3 are essential. The rest are recommended, although you can lose features or slow access to the meeting.

1. Update to the latest version:

Whether you are using the application for Windows, iOS or Android, you must have the latest version installed. Zoom has run its batteries and will remind you every time you walk in and haven't done the last update.

2. Install an antivirus:

Whatever your operating system, you should have a paid antivirus, if possible. You pay hundreds of euros to buy it and zero to protect it. The content is more important than the device itself.

3. Add a meeting password

When you create a meeting, Zoom generates a new default ID and adds a password. Both measures are perfect to protect you from intruders.

4. Enable a waiting room

This way, you can filter access. The host has to allow or deny each participant's access. If it is a mass meeting, this option will not be feasible.

5. Make registration compulsory

Everyone who attends the meeting will have to enter their name and email. Also, there will be a record of the time you have arrived. Very useful also for roll call.

6. Avoid using your meeting room

It is your room and is associated with your identity within Zoom (ID), so it never changes. This makes it more vulnerable since if someone finds out, they can enter whenever they want. If you have not started a meeting, there is no problem but if you just enter when you are in a sales session it can seriously harm you. Zoom has noticed and now it is mandatory to establish a password to access your room.

7. Turn off file transfer

This option is available in the paid versions. Allows you to transfer files between participants. If you are going to use it, do not deactivate it. You can also share files by uploading them to a cloud service (Dropbox, Google Drive) and pasting the link.

There are other additional steps you can take once you have started a meeting. They are found in the bottom bar, on the Security tab:

Lock Meeting: Restrict access to new participants.

Enable waiting room: As mentioned, each participant requires that you allow them to access the meeting.

Screen Sharing: Activate or deactivate this option for participants.

That the name be changed: This way you can identify those present.

Chat: You can disable the chat entirely to be attended to.

As you can see, there are many steps you can take to make your meeting a safe place. The essentials are to update to the latest version, install an antivirus and set a password to enter the meeting.

ADVANTAGES AND DISADVANTAGES

Zoom is one of the most quickly increasing video conferencing technologies out there. Installation and hosting of video calls are fast. It is perfect for video chats with friends and family or conferencing with your staff when operating from home. There are many benefits of using Zoom in your teaching and remote working in this scenario.

Benefits of Zoom

Unless the business is like the other, all of its workers are operating right now from home because of the current scenario worldwide. It will usually find teamwork incredibly challenging. Software solutions such as Zoom, however, communicate nature and extent. You might use Zoom to hold a community meeting with all of your staff regardless of where each participant is. Additionally, you can hold one-on-one meetings, workshops for employee training, and more through the Zoom website. Such critical technologies make it easier for management practitioners to link and involve their diverse teams and keep their businesses going productively forward.

Zoom has several useful functionality tools. Yet fortunately, because of the elegant Zoom design, these functions are simple to use. Many of the features of the video conferencing system are readily available. They need limited instruction to allow full use of them. When you want to get lost, the Zoom page provides loads of support tools. Finally, Zoom is helpful because it does not charge you to use your corporation. It is pretty cheap, in fact, regarding the abundance of characteristics it comes with. You can use functions for free though Zoom still provides premium plans with comprehensive feature sets. But even these are not going to make any difference, ensuring good return on investment for the organizations that use it.

Remote Working

We are trying to maintain things stable while the condition is not usually challenging-particularly during global crises. One such thing is to change roles and work from home while we are used to going to the workplace every day. In these days of video calling, tweeting, and file sharing, several people are happily willing to transfer their workdays early. Nonetheless, remote work has been a part of the daily lifestyle of many cultures for years. Although the transition may seem challenging, it is not impossible. Developers take on our staff's technology strategies and the knowledge of many of our reporters and editors to put together information and suggestions from home on having worked. It involves both detailed information about working remotely, having to deal with conference calls, and make a decent standing desk, but also quick tips on how to utilize Zoom. Zoom can help in organizing class meetings and staff meetings sitting at home. It can help you to work remotely no matter where you are and what you are doing.

Work from Home

Remote job and teaching more effective are becoming increasingly common in schools and businesses worldwide, and institutions need to ensure their employees have the techniques they need to get the best communications experience at home. Zoom is introducing the unveiling of the latest category, Zoom, for Home, as part of our commitment to helping anyone operating from home, enabling you to access a dedicated personal communication tool for video presentations, phone calls, and immersive whiteboard. Each group incorporates updates to the Zoom app with compatible equipment for improving the home business experience.

Zoom for Home is also compliant with all Zoom Rooms Devices, like Sleek and Poly hardware options, enabling consumers to pick the equipment they need to build the ideal work-from, home connectivity experience through spaces including the family room. Sign in to a computer compliant with Zoom for Home with a Zoom user profile to immediately create interactive office environments with no additional licenses (Zoom for Home is eligible for all Zoom discussion licenses, except Basic).

• Easily schedule meetings, work collaboratively virtually with information sharing and annotation and send and receive telephone calls.

• Synchronizes with the user's schedule, status, conference settings, and phone for an embedded video-first identity management experience.

• Zoom for home computers may be established for virtual IT control through the admin app.

• Ensures the equipment is primarily developed for simple operation with minimal or no IT assistance is suited for desk configurations and matches the price level for setting up a home workplace.

A Chance to Work on your Passion

If you should do one thing to change your life, it is doing what you are excited about and using it as a profession, as a career, or as a passion. While this is not easy, the path is worth it because it pays off when you are doing something that you enjoy. It is not easy to work on your passion while attending a hectic routine. A tiring job or a student routine can make you keep your passion aside. During the current scenario, there is a lot of time for everyone to take a stand and work hard on passion while staying at home using Zoom. It can help you to learn different things and taking classes in different short courses. Zoom provides excellent benefits for its users, especially in the learning process.

Good for Online Teaching

As a teacher, if you or your learners have a situation that keeps you from meeting the person, Zoom can help maintain your class going. Online class meetings, in which everyone is planned to join a Zoom meeting, are one way to create interaction when learners are remote. Still, Zoom can also be used to assist other learning and teaching situations. So long as a student attendant is on a laptop, they can select a connection to the URL and be taken to a chat with the instructor instantly. It removes slow updates entirely, annoying bonus services, and plenty of boring things. Often people need to upgrade their software or flash to reach, but that never transforms into an issue that lasts more than two minutes. It is suitable for first-time gatherings and already-off meetings. Zoom provides different beneficial features for online classes like a whiteboard, screen sharing, screen recording, assignment and presentation setup, etc.

ZOOM SAFETY

Is it safe to utilize the videoconferencing application Zoom? Indeed, on the off chance that you realize how to set it up appropriately.

To start with, some foundation. As you may know, Zoom's fame has emerged over the recent months as individuals are approached to remain at home, you can utilize its free form to keep in contact with companions, family, and associates.

In any case, while Zoom previously incorporated a few techniques that could be utilized to shield gatherings, those highlights could be elusive, mainly if you hadn't utilized the application previously. Along these lines, gatherings started to be hindered by undesirable gatecrashers. They might intentionally cause interruptions, frequently in incredibly frightful ways.

Of course, this prompted an impressive kickback, quite a bit concerning the absence of security for clients. Accordingly, the organization has set up extra safety efforts. For instance, it's consequently empowering virtual sitting areas and passwords for accounts in its free and most minimal paid levels.

Managing passwords and virtual lounge areas may make for a marginally less friendly interface. Yet, it additionally implies that it's more outlandish someone you don't realize will fly into your family get-together. Along these lines, in case you're utilizing the free form of Zoom, here are a few different ways to keep your gatherings secure.

Utilize A Unique Meeting Id and Password

Zoom is presently naturally adding passwords to accounts, and those passwords can be installed in the connections to individuals' very own rooms.

Anybody you send that connect to will have the option to promptly access your gathering without having to post a secret key independently. Posting that interface freely will discredit any security the secret key may have given.

Thus, in case you're making a gathering for more than a few companions, it's presumably a smart thought not to utilize your typical gathering ID and to create a different secret key. To do that utilizing the web interface:

• From the entire Zoom page, click on "My Account" in the upper-right corner, and afterward click "Timetable a gathering."

• If you like, you could enter a gathering theme and portrayal. Put in the date, time, and length of your gathering. (In case you're on the free arrangement, you will be given 40 minutes.)

• Look for "Meeting ID" and select "Create Automatically." This will produce a novel ID for that gathering instead of utilization your typical gathering ID.

• Make sure "Require a secret phrase" is checked. Zoom will produce an odd secret word, yet you can likewise make your own.

• Below that, ensure "Empower lounge area" is checked (and it's a smart thought not to check "Empower join before have" since that would let members meander into the gathering before you do).

72

- Click on "Spare."

- You'll be brought to the gatherings page where you will see the entirety of the choices for that gathering. Mostly down, you can click "Duplicate the greeting" to place the entirety of the data into your cradle so you can send it to your members. At the point when you're prepared, click on the blue "Start this Meeting" button.

- In case You're Using the Zoom App:

- Click on "Time."

- You will be offered indistinguishable choices from the web application. Click on "Cutting edge Options" at the base of the page.

- Click on the blue "Calendar" button

- You'll be offered the opportunity to place the gathering into your schedule. From that point onward, you'll be taken back to the primary window. The planned gathering will be on the right; on the off chance that you need, you can tap on the three dabs to one side of your name to make changes or duplicate the greeting into a cushion to send to your members.

Utilize the Virtual Waiting Room

Of equivalent or significantly more use is the virtual lounge area. This lets you look at everybody before they access the gathering. You can then either give them access — or not.

At the point when every member tap on their connection, they will be approached to pause. At the same time, you will get a notice revealing to you that somebody has gone into the sitting area. You can either concede them in a split second or tap on "See sitting area."

A sidebar will, at that point, give you every individual who is standing by to enter the gathering; you can then either concede them, expel them from the lounge area (and from any opportunity to enter the gathering), or send them a message.

Affirming each individual who needs to join may be an agony to manage, particularly if you're anticipating many individuals; however, it will guarantee that any individual who appears in your gathering has a place there.

Lock Down, Don't Share, Kick Them Out

Other securities include that you can exploit to ensure yourself and different members.

You can secure the gathering by tapping on the "Security" connect at the base of the screen and picking "Lock Meeting." Once you do that, even someone who has the gathering ID and secret word can't get in.

Utilizing a similar menu, it could likewise be a smart thought, particularly in case you're holding a gathering with many individuals, unchecking the "Offer Screen" determination. On the off chance that by misfortune, someone who intends to disturb the gathering is permitted to share their screen, they can make things amazingly awkward for the remainder of the members. (If sooner or later, a member has an authentic need to share their screen, you can reenable sharing whenever.)

On the off chance that a member begins to get out of hand, however you would prefer not to show them out (or you need to talk about what you will get them for their birthday), you can return them in the sitting area.

Snap-on, the "Oversee Participants" symbol at the base of your screen, discover the name of the member on the subsequent sideboard, and afterward click on "Additional" > "Put the member in the lounge area." With this, the member will no longer approach the gathering room or meeting; in influence, they will stay in the sitting area until you choose to permit them to return.

You can show someone out of the gathering entirely by utilizing that equivalent drop-down menu and tapping on "Evacuate." If that gets vital, incidentally, it may be a smart thought to bolt the gathering then so they can't attempt to get back in.

USING ZOOM ON PHONE

This part shows you how to set up Zoom on your android and iOS phones. You can join gatherings, talk with contacts, and view an index of contacts, utilizing the Zoom Cloud

Open the Zoom application

- Sign in to your record to utilize all highlights.

- After marking in, click on 'Meet and talk' to get to the accompanying highlights:

- Start meeting - This permits you to begin a moment meeting utilizing your PMI or a New Meeting ID.

- Join - Using the gathering ID, join a gathering

- Schedule - Plan a repetitive or a one-time meeting.

- Upcoming gatherings - Start, alter, see, or erase your planned Zoom gatherings.

- Click your 'name' to utilize your own talk space.

Phone

Telephone - Tap 'telephone' to get to Zoom telephone highlights (a permit is required).

Keypad - Contact or call a number creation utilization of organization number or direct telephone number.

History tab - Check your call log to show replied, recorded, and missed calls.

Voice message tab - Delete and play phone message messages.

Contacts

Snap 'contacts' to list every one of your contacts and include new ones.

Registry tab - Click 'the contact' to initiate a one-on-one visit with them.

Channels tab - Enables you to get to a rundown of open, private, and featured channels.

Zoom Rooms tab - Check a rundown of Zoom Rooms. Snap a 'Zoom Room' to begin a gathering with it.

Settings

•   Snap 'settings' to see gatherings and visit settings.

•   Snap 'your name' to change your name, secret key, and profile picture.

Contacts - Search telephone contacts that are zoom clients and support contact demands.

Meeting-Alter when you are advised of new messages by zoom.

Telephone View direct telephone number and friends' number.

Visit Enable or impair connect see in talk messages.

About zoom - Access the application form and send your input.

Instructions to enable zoom

•   Dispatch the Settings application on your home screen

- Snap-on 'General'

- Snap-on 'Openness'

- Snap 'Zoom' under the Vision segment

- Snap the 'Change' to turn on Zoom.

You can utilize it in a hurry when you got it empowered. Here are the rules for you:

- Double-tap with three fingers anyplace on the screen to either empower or handicap Zoom. This should be possible anyplace

- Drag three fingers around the screen and play around with it to another region of the screen.

- Use a couple of fingers to look in the specific segment that is on the screen.

- Click and wait on the 'grapple' to drag the glass all over the screen.

The most effective method to enable/disable the Zoom Controller

This permits you to dish around a zoomed-in part of the screen and quickly zoom in and out. You turn it on by:

Launching settings from your home screen

- Snap 'general.'

- Snap 'openness'

- Tap 'zoom'

- Snap the 'switch' close to 'show controller.'

Step by step instructions to Change Region

You can choose to Zoom inside a moveable window or on the general screen. This should be possible by:

- Launching settings from your home screen

- Snap 'general.'

- Snap 'availability'

- Tap 'zoom'

- Snap 'zoom locale'

- Snap either 'full-screen zoom' or 'window zoom'.

Step by step instructions to change the filter

Maybe you need the hues applied on the zoomed-in territory, or you need low light; you can get these choices enacted, and they will apply to what in particular is in the zoom region.

- Launch settings from your home screen

- Snap 'general'

- Snap 'availability'

- Snap 'zoom'

- Snap 'zoom channel'

- Snap 'a choice':

- None

- Modified

- Grayscale

- Grayscale modified

- Low light.

Step by step instructions to change the maximum level

- Launch Settings from your home screen

- Snap 'general.'

- Snap 'availability'

- Snap 'zoom'

- Snap and move the 'slider' under the most extreme zoom level.

Step by step instructions to change controller visibility

At the point when the show controller is turned on, you can control how straightforward the zoom controller is.

- Launch Settings from your home screen

- Snap 'general.'

- Snap 'openness'

- Snap 'zoom'

- Snap 'shroud perceivability'

- Snap and hang on the 'slider' and move it to change the controller perceivability. To make it more obvious, drag to one side. To make it less noticeable, drag it to one side.

RECORDING IN ZOOM

It tends to be hard to recollect each point examined during a gathering, particularly on the off chance that you secured more than one theme. Rather than taking notes, you can record Zoom gatherings and watch them when you need significant data.

Also, recording a Zoom meeting will permit you to talk about subtleties to your associates who couldn't go to the gathering. You don't need to be comfortable with the innovation to record a Zoom meeting, because a video recording meeting can begin or stop with a solitary snap.

Record A Zoom Meeting from A Mac or Pc

At the point when you need a gathering recording, Zoom has two different ways to pick. The free and paid forms of Zoom give a neighborhood recording highlight that permits clients to store recorded clasps on their nearby hard drives. Free neighborhood enrollment is given. While comparing cloud enlistment is accessible at a beginning cost of $ 14.99/mo./star size host, it functions admirably for little groups. With a modest size business beginning with ten has, this offer is $ 19.99/mo. For business. At long last, the most elevated offer is Enterprise for $ 19.99/mo./100 have for the most prominent association.

You ought to determine the envelope where your document will be spared before beginning a gathering recording to abstain from scanning for the organizer that is consequently made for this reason.

In the wake of running the Zoom Desktop Client, you should tap on the settings symbol to get to the settings window.

Go to the "Recording" tab and snap the "Open" button close to the "Spare chronicles to" alternative. (Note: in Windows, you will consider it to be neighborhood recording). Alternatively, you can likewise empower video recording while at the same time sharing the screen.

You should ensure that the nearby chronicle choice is empowered before you can begin recording a gathering. Go to the Personal List and snap on the Settings tab to check if the neighborhood enlistment highlight is debilitated.

Snap the switch button close to the nearby log choice if the component isn't actuated.

Zoom additionally permits you to empower this component on all gatherings you make with it. Snap-on, the Group Management symbol, discover the gathering you need to empower this choice and go to the Settings tab. Open the Registration tab and empower the neighborhood enrollment choice if it is impaired.

You can empower the neighborhood logging alternative by clicking My Meeting Settings. At the same time, account individuals can play out this errand from the Meeting Settings menu. In either case, you should open the Registry tab and afterward check that the Local Registry choice is empowered.

Record Local Zoom Meetings

Start the Zoom meeting when you're prepared and tap the record button. On the off chance that a menu shows up on your screen, you should pick the account alternative on this PC, and a little chronicle tape will be shown in the lower right corner of your screen.

After stopping the account, Zoom will change over the gathering recording with the goal that the document is open.

Once the chronicle is finished, the record will be changed over and spared in the .mp4 group. The recorded documents will likewise show up in the Zoom envelope.

Can't you find your record? Open the program, find and snap the gathering. Select the recorded choice; when opened, you will locate the recorded documents.

Managing recorded documents is straightforward. You can decide to open the document, play the recorded video legitimately, or play just the sound.

Record A Rounding Meeting with Third-Party Software: Aura Scrun On a Windows And Mac Computers

One of the alternatives is to utilize Fillmore scorn to record a zoom meeting, mainly when you can't record zoom gatherings with the implicit zoom device. Regardless of whether in a little gathering or for a more immense scope, this alternative gives another approach to exploit Windows and Mac frameworks.

First of all, download and introduce Filmora scrn.

Once the program begins, you should pick "Start" to begin recording on the off chance that you need to get the full settings.

You have four choices around there: screen, sound, camera, and chimney. METER. If you have to utilize the sound, pick the alternative you pick by tapping on the symbol. Finish the progression by clicking Settings to make any alterations before recording starts.

At this point, select the video of the gathering with zoom and begin recording by clicking "catch." You will get a commencement from 3 to 1.

Immediately after the tally is finished, press F10 to quit recording. Or then again, tweak a snappy on/off switch in the arrangement menu. At the point when complete, the document will be put in the library where you can choose it for additional altering or offer it if incredible.

Record Zoom Meeting from iPhone Or Android

It is absurd to expect to record gatherings locally from iPhone and Android gadgets. You should buy one of the free memberships that intends to get to Zoom's cloud enlistment highlight. With the cloud enrollment alternative, you can share, see or download records legitimately from your Zoom account.

Snap-on the More symbol when you start a gathering from your iPhone and pick the cloud recording choice from the menu.

The account bar will show up in the upper right corner of your screen to illuminate you that the chronicle meeting is in progress. You can interruption or respite the account by tapping on the More symbol, and your recordings will be put in a My Recordings organizer that can be gotten to from an internet browser.

The way toward recording a Zoom meeting from an Android telephone is like the one simply portrayed. When the Zoom meeting begins, you have to tap on the More symbol and pick the account choice. Snap-on a similar symbol at whatever point you need to delay or respite an account meeting and go to the My Recordings envelope to review the video you made.

Record Texts

Notwithstanding recording Zoom gatherings, you can likewise naturally duplicate the gathering sound that you record in the cloud. As the host of the gathering, you can alter the content, filter the content for watchwords to get to the video now, and offer the account. Pick Activate, if vital. On the off chance that the alternative is dormant, it is bolted at the gathering or record level, and you should contact your Zoom overseer.

THE ESSENTIAL QUALITY OF AN ONLINE TEACHER

In the ordinary sense, teaching involves formal lessons on a theme, usually together with a close lesson and strategies of assessment.

Teacher as Leader

Leadership comprises those items that require the teacher's interaction or involvement in ways other than content area instruction—educating others about online learning, modeling best practices for colleagues, active participation in professional networks, and active engagement in policy initiatives.

Designer of Learning Experiences

Whether you design the entire curriculum for a course you teach, or you teach using a prepackaged curriculum, you are the deliverer of the content. You alone determine how your learners will engage with you, with each other, and with the content. It is up to you to know and understand the pedagogical approaches and strategies that are most effective for any given online lesson, including which tools are most appropriate for delivering that content.

A supporter of the Learning Community

The emphasis on community building in the standards is not an accident. It has become evident that engaging and supportive online learning communities create more engaged learners and produce better outcomes. And yes, collaboration is an essential element in building significant learning communities and facilitating online environments.

Facilitator

Facilitators are the process flow designers. They manage the flow of discussion boards, the feedback loop, allow for the free and organized flow of information, and redirect it when learning is off-task. In effect, they orchestrate every process in the learning experience. Good facilitation takes practice, but can more easily be learned through modeling.

Data Analyst

Data in online environments are plentiful and can be entirely meaningful. Of course, data can consist of formative and summative assessments. Still, in an LMS, data can also consist of user tracking through visualized interfaces and dashboards. Data should be used to guide instruction and to inform parents and other stakeholders about what is working and what is not working. The good news about online teaching is that everything is transparent in an LMS. It is the perfect platform for data-driven collaboration and decision-making processes.

Educator

Facilitating an online course is both similar to and different from traditional classroom instruction. Helping learners understand the subject matter, engaging them in critical thinking through questioning, and providing support to them are necessary skills for all teachers. These tasks are accomplished in the online classroom; however, they can be vastly different from in a traditional classroom. Online communication is conducted through text-based communication tools such as e-mail, chat rooms, and threaded discussion forums. Instructors need a certain level of creativity to create an environment that is safe, inviting, motivating, and engaging when they are not physically present. Commonplace verbal forms of communication are absent.

Project Manager

If you approach teaching from a traditional, teacher-centered, behaviorist viewpoint—as most of us have in the past—you should be prepared to change. Standards and guidelines on effective online teaching advocates are creating student-centered learning environments. Research supports collaborative inquiry, community building, and interaction as vehicles for promoting learner motivation and engagement in online classes.

Instructional Designer

The amount of time devoted to instructional design will depend on many factors (e.g., grade level, content area, school or program policies, etc.). Regardless, the ability to design instruction is a valuable and necessary skill, whether you teach in a face-to-face or online environment. Being an influential instructional designer requires not only knowledge and skill in the development and design of the classroom and curriculum, but also requires the ability to recognize when and how specific strategies and content are appropriate and effective.

Preparations for the online classroom include setting objectives, gathering materials, writing explanations, creating assessments, and designing multimedia presentations to illustrate complex concepts. Even when using a prepackaged curriculum, the instructor prepares in advance by becoming familiar with the content, activities, and expected student outcomes. The expected amount of activity between the instructor and the learners and peer-to-peer interactions will also influence the course design.

E-Learning Expert

Troubleshooting falls within the realm of this competency and therefore is a crucial skill for online instructors. Of course, you cannot know every issue that your students might encounter, but you can prepare for some common difficulties. For example, when learners experience problems logging into your classroom, having a list of fixes will come in handy.

Compassionate

Compassion begins in the soil of patience and connection, but it grows beyond that as well. I think it assumes the best. Something is disarming about compassion. The negligent student is often more responsive to kindness than to rigidness. Moreover, compassion does not preclude being firm. We can follow our kindness with exact and firm requirements.

Good Listener

The excellent online teacher is remembered because of their willingness to listen. But how do you listen online? Have you ever made a hasty reply to an email to find out later that you had read the email too fast and missed something important? It is easy to do. Online listening often means setting aside emails until you have time to give them your full attention.

Flexible

It is a difficult one because there are always those students, to whom if you give an inch, they will take a mile. We fear that if we push out an assignment date, our students will stop taking due dates seriously. A massive wave of late assignments will then crash onto our desk during the final weeks of the course. The good news is that your course design and syllabus provide you with a lot of structure to lean on, making you flexible. Sometimes you may need your students to be flexible with you. That was the case for me this semester.

In your online course, that also means creating avenues of communication with your students, where they have opportunities to discuss, ask questions, and share their lives with you. That connection is your fuel to excellence as an online instructor.

To sum that up: it is all about teaching habits. Those habits are built on the structures you put in place, and your habits are fueled by the connection you develop with your learners.

The world of online education may be one of the most rapidly changing fields of our day. Because of that, this book will focus on more enduring topics, like habits, structures, and connections.

In considering online teaching, you may feel as if you are heading into unchartered waters. It might be helpful to compare teaching online to teaching in a brick-and-mortar setting.

As an online instructor, you must be willing to release some control, to encourage a learning community that empowers the learner. It is the most challenging transition that some instructors make, and some make it more quickly than others. With this loss of control, there comes the recognition that the strategies you are most comfortable and thriving within the face-to-face classroom do not work in the online classroom.

ZOOM VS. MICROSOFT TEAMS

Which is better with Microsoft Teams versus Zoom? As the UC showcase is moving continuously from UC to UCaaS, the primary serious situation that most clients are bantering with us is no longer Skype for Business versus Cisco, yet the cloud situation (which presently includes both video conferencing and sound, with a beginning (Zoom Phone usefulness) of Zoom versus Microsoft Teams in the cloud, and with regards to contrasting Microsoft Teams versus Zoom, the arrangement is similarly as precarious in the cutting edge UCaaS condition now as it was in the old fight among Microsoft and Cisco.

Every one of these moderately new stages has seen a quick turn of events, gathering a significant number of highlights and fans. Try not to squint; the progressing rivalry, creation, and satisfaction of new situations for end-client and endeavor satisfaction are probably going to be quick-fire over in any event the following scarcely any years.

Numerous organizations are at present in the Skype for Business blend. In any case, with the ongoing declaration of the finish of-life date for Skype for Business Online (and the hypothesis that the on-prem version would have a comparable destiny), it is provoking numerous IT groups to determine what their subsequent stage will be for their biological system of availability and participation.

So how would you settle on Zoom and Microsoft Teams? First, take a gander at the separate of every stage and afterward jump into comparing them as close as possible to a level playing field.

How are Microsoft Teams?

Microsoft Teams is the widely inclusive work stream joint effort with Microsoft in addition to a brought together correspondences stage – interfacing gatherings, calls, visits, and record offer to the Office 365 application stack to unite everybody in a shared workspace.

Breakdown of the Microsoft Teams Vs. Zoom

Microsoft Teams and Zoom both meet and contend significantly by giving a scope of video conferencing devices (counting room frameworks) and UC communication administrations. Soft more top to bottom into the more mind-boggling usefulness, Usability, evaluating, and arrangement is how organizations can decide compromises and settle on the correct choices concerning which stage is the match.

1) Characteristics

Where applications are concerned, both Zoom and Teams permit online gatherings, discussions, calls, screen sharing, and document sharing. Microsoft's cooperation of Teams and its Office 365 stage is the distinction between the two. This makes it workable for Microsoft Teams to be a one-stop-look for some associations. This additionally permits consistent, coordinated effort, reinforcements, and the quest for documents. In any case, going some approach to supplement the consolidation of Microsoft's Office365, Zoom and Slack highlights a wide-going relationship and an assortment of innovative blends.

Zoom, as an association, is a much more current association than Microsoft's behemoth. However, it prompts rivaling its forceful guide, and because it doesn't need to stress over overseeing (and in the end leaving) a lot of inheritance clients at the premises.

2) UX (Utility Interface)

In Microsoft Teams versus Zoom banter, the UI and experience are really where Zoom exceeds expectations. Zoom clients are, for the most part raving about its straightforward interface and the capacity to get end clients fully operational with restricted to no preparation or IT support.

Microsoft Teams face a more significant test as clients need to get to grasp with how to impart in different systems and groups, incorporate document sharing, just as the other Office 365 applications incorporated with groups. Although the full scope of intuitive work stream highlights incorporated with Teams empowers it to give a more extensive field of utilization and situations (and along these lines a more noteworthy worth) than Zoom, this particular degree is likewise, in specific regards, its Achilles heel as respects on board.

3) Room Systems

At the point when territories of the field Zoom versus Groups keep on turning out to be exceptionally commoditized, one field of remarkable qualification is the "space frameworks" that are worked inside an undertaking. A room format can go from a fundamental arrangement of the cluster space to a particular meeting space for chiefs. Albeit both give application control, contact redesigns, versatile friend cooperation's, and double screen room support, Zoom has the additional bit of leeway of tallying individuals, and Teams have vicinity discovery. Another differentiation among Zoom and Microsoft Teams is that Zoom confirms all integrators and equipment providers. In contrast, just the equipment arrangements are affirmed by Teams.

4) Pricing

Microsoft Teams and Zoom offer each a free form of the stage, offering further developed highlights with paid plans.

Microsoft Teams Free form incorporates limited visits and coordinated effort, applications, and administrations for profitability, gatherings, calls, and security. Two enormous pieces that are absent with the free form incorporate organization instruments or backing from Microsoft.

The free form of Zoom incorporates gatherings that can have up to 100 members (with a gathering meeting breaking point of 40 minutes), boundless 1:1 gatherings, online help, video and web conferencing highlights, bunch cooperation highlights, and security.

Microsoft's Premium arrangement is insignificantly less expensive per client than the proportionate Pro arrangement for Zoom; however, they are valued similarly with their corporate plans.

5) UC Telephony

The capacity to make calls at an undertaking level is significant, particularly for video, sound, conferencing, and informing business interchanges. This sort of highlight has at first been a fortress of Microsoft, as Zoom didn't at first have a telephone framework item.

The Zoom Telephone is the endeavor voice reaction. The advanced and quickly developing cloud telephone framework offers shrewd call steering and the board, auto-chaperon/IVR, interoperability with ordinary endpoints like voice message, call history, guest ID, and portable dialing to call recording. As with Microsoft Teams, it offers the product on both work areas and cell phones. Besides, Zoom's "Present to Your Own Carrier" framework is an immediate reaction to the Direct Routing capacity of Teams, empowering Zoom Phone associations to utilize built up PSTN specialist co-ops in numerous world markets.

6) Zoom Debate

The most tremendous success for Microsoft Teams is its tight, prepared in combination with Office 365 applications. In any case, past that, Microsoft Teams have more than 70 mixes that incorporate ticket the board alternatives, surveys, climate, news, etc.

Incorporations, for the most part, on account of Microsoft, are too placed client information into its system. On the other side, the Zoom is frequently added to different stages as a joining. One extraordinary case of this is how Slack and Zoom work aggregately.

Notwithstanding the Slack blend, Zoom has more than 100 mixes, including an Office 365 combination.

Zoom and Teams: If you are thinking about the two frameworks running simultaneously, you would require a typical administration system that works for both. It is only that Power Suite does!

In actuality, on the two Teams and Zoom, we are progressively observing huge organizations deciding to "normalize." Microsoft Teams are great for coordinated interior effort. However, Zoom is regularly favored for outer work, with clients or visitor merchants. Since they speak with each other, it is straightforward for clients to construct explicit situations in which to utilize when.

Multiplatform in the new advanced workforce is turning out to be perpetually the current norm. An examination found in an ongoing overview that 85 per cent of clients utilize various stages for shared applications.

THE FUTURE OF VIDEO CONFERENCING

Why Video Conferencing Is Better Than Phonecalls/ Emails

(a.k.a the reason why not everyone who reads the Gettysburg Address sounds like Abraham Lincoln)

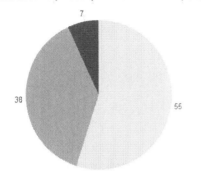

- Percentage Impact of Words in Communicating Intention, Assuming a Common Language
- Percentage Impact of Tone of Voice in Communicating Intention, Assuming a Common Language
- Percentage Impact of Facial Expression in Communicating Intention, Assuming a Common Language

Risk Management Vs. Forward-Thinking

Switching to new technology or new methods of working can be daunting. However, while change carries an active risk, it is also true that stagnation carries a risk of its own.

While reading this book, you may have noted that while it has been helpful. For this reason, you'll never know me if I walk down the street, nor do you necessarily feel any particular kinship toward me - it'd take many, many more books for that.

Compare and contrast to meeting face-to-face. You might decide within fifteen seconds that you like someone, or will get along with them. All this is made possible through visual communication and body language. Videoconferencing is what allows you to retain this powerful force multiplier across vast distances.

If your business relies a lot on travelling for meeting purposes, I strongly recommend you upgrade to at least a basic version of Zoom. Not only does it save you fuel and accommodation costs, but it can also earn you brownie points with environmentalists for some neat PR as you can (truthfully) claim you use videoconferencing to reduce the waste that so often plagues the excessive catering, disposable cups, crumpled papers and other derelict leftovers generated by traditional meetings.

In a world where we grapple with inflation and potential resource scarcity, videoconferencing could buy time needed to reach the next innovative idea and will save you plenty of money regardless. Even Zoom's most expensive plan, at $19.99 per host, per month, is often cheaper than the average $100 cost per person per night for a hotel stay in the U.S.A. (Lock, 2020).

Hardware & Tech

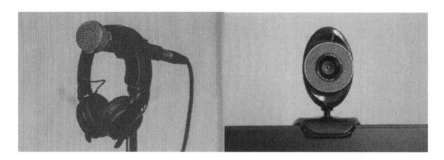

The more you rely on video conferencing, the more you should consider investing in better audio-visual equipment. A lousy microphone can make you sound soft, or drown the meeting in a low humming drone. A mediocre microphone might add a little fuzziness to your voice, or cut out from time to time, necessitating repetition and ruining your annunciation, all of which make it harder for you to be understood.

Meanwhile, operating without a webcam can negate the entire point of using videoconferencing; without video, you may as well take a phone-call or write an email for all the good it does. A low webcam, meanwhile, can cause much of the subtlety in your expressions to be lost, and no one likes looking at an overly-blurry or pixelated image.

If you find yourself experiencing these issues, no matter how you tweak your audio or video settings, strongly consider upgrading so that your face can appear bright and vivid, your voice crisp and clear. Suppose you are incredibly important to the meeting in some other way (e.g., if a group of the management staff is interviewing you to see if you can meet a job's requirements, you are where all the attention will be, so you'll want to make sure your tech isn't holding back your neatness and presentation). You especially don't want to sound muffled, robotic, and squeaky when you speak, so certainly invest in an external microphone for a more organic, deep, and rich-sounding video-conferencing voice.

External microphones and webcams are always recommended over integrated ones due to nearly always being of significantly better quality. For a reliable hardware provider, try Logitech for microphones, webcams, and even headsets.

Location, Location, Location

Aside from purchasing additional hardware, you can also improve the professionalism of your presentation through a few simple tricks.

For your webcam, the general rule is to set it just above your eye-level, facing you at a subtle downwards angle. Setting it lower than this might make you look arrogant, uncanny, or boorish while setting it higher than making you seem puny. When set just right, you will look approachable, but not ignorable. Pay attention to the angle from which entertainers and film stars are viewed during their most dynamic and glamorous close-ups.

For optimal lighting that accentuates the life in your face, consider placing a working daylight bulb around 4 feet away from your webcam to the left and right on either side. Clamp lights are best for this, but floor or table lamps will do in a pinch.

Next, to improve the acoustics in your room with little-to-no budget, drape thick curtains over all windows in your room to decrease reverberation caused by the glass. Placing your props or furniture to occupy the corners of your room will also prevent more resonant sounds from building up too firmly.

To ensure that wind (or even your breathing) does not disrupt or distort your speech, it's also highly recommended that you invest in a microphone windshield or pop-filter, even if it's just a cheap or basic one, as the difference compared to not using one at all can be huge. Finally, to guarantee your voice is captured perfectly from this point on, always be sure to speak directly into your microphone as placing it even a few inches too far can cause your voice to become unbearably soft.

BUILD REAL CONNECTION TO YOUR STUDENTS

Eligible online educators often worry that virtual teaching is more about making a good learning experience and not just about the mechanics of distance learning—no matter what the setting of learning is. Despite that, getting to know their students is very challenging for some online teachers. It happens when an online class has 20 and above students at a time. So, if the course is online, with no eye to eye connections, how can you build individual connections? There are various proven ways to work around the issue. I pulled up some of them to help you navigate building connections with your students.

As an online instructor, building a strong connection with your students is crucial because there is no visual aid to help you see all of them at once during a class. While a couple of the students in the class are noisy, they may stay quiet.

Thus, it turns out to be extremely difficult for you to know which student is doing some other thing, sleeping, incapable of seeing the course layout, or just generally lost. It happens in an online course that neglects to include a vital learning key, i.e., personal connection with the instructor.

Without a vital connection with you, your students can get confused and may feel detached. It makes them less motivated, and they begin to lose interest in the course.

Principles

Online classes can be a lot like conventional study halls in which a couple of students do a large portion of the talking, and others never make a single sound. When a course is 100% online with no eye to eye contact, what principles would you apply to cause individual connections to occur? Try out one-on-one communication options

Setting up these connections on an individual level requires some effort. Here are some credible methods you can try:

• Introductions: Most online courses include a type of early introduction, for example, a conversation discussion that expects students to post something important to them to get to know one another better.

• Discussion Boards: This may not be possible to react to each student's post each week. This methodology isn't desirable, either. They may give you another way of concentrating on different individual students every week.

• Email: All over your course, there are various points when you or your students have to start an email discussion. It can be an excellent way to check on a student when you notice there have not been active or he/she is missing assignments.

• Make it meaningful: A personal connection with your students is a higher priority than creative conversations. Everyone is occupied with responsibilities of work, school, and family, so adding prerequisites for connection for the sake of just adding them is counterproductive.

• Consider class size and time: Be realistic about what you can achieve, given the number of students in your course and the amount of time you need to work with them. Extensive registrations, as well as shorter learning times, make individual connections nearly impossible. Alter your expectations appropriately and consider what you can do with little groups to cultivate a connection and communication.

• Plan ahead: Make plans to learn and adapt for both you and your students and continue working on transparent communication systems.

• Practice: Challenge yourself to make these individual connections, yet allow time for slow adaptation. Start gradually with new methods to know what works for you and your students, and don't be hesitant to get some information about their interests and expectations. The same way you adjust your content and materials before every lesson, you can also try new ways to communicate.

Small Teaching Online Quick Tip: Building Connections

Here are a few tips for building connections with your students:

Introduce Yourself

Create a feeling of cooperation and connection between your students and yourself by starting the first conversation. Try to make this meeting by inspiring conversation regarding the learning and individual goals of students, their strengths, and other additional characteristics.

You can begin by posting a short bio of yourself. It may include your area of specialization, background, interests, and your most recent photograph. It will make your students feel that you are a good teacher, and they will follow your example and use it to guide them in sharing information about themselves with the rest of the class.

It is one of the best ways to connect with the students in your online classroom and to know their interests. You can also use Google Forms to gather information on your students, find out about their interests, their background, their educational abilities, and their learning preferences. Another smart idea is to dedicate a particular part of your course site for posting pictures and brief profiles of all of your students.

Or then again, even better, you can ask your students to create a quick personal mindset board that they can share with you and the rest of the class. For this, you ask them to use a few accessible online mindset mapping instruments.

Adapt Your Course

One of the best ways to amplify the individual connection and expand the capability of eLearning is to adapt your course. When we say adapt the course, we mean structure it in a way that incorporates human connection.

An adapted course is bound to establish a relationship between you and your students, and this can be accomplished in the following ways:

Influence Online Conversations

Give the students a conversation platform. Providing an online conversation board contributes to relating with friends and fellow students and in getting important feedback. Because of this, the best choice is to go with an online platform that you are familiar with— one which is easily reachable to your students. Additionally, you can use the conversation boards' tool, or perhaps you can create a Facebook group and ask your students to join.

Advance Multimedia with Personalization

Media fused courses empower the various kinds of students to meet their personal needs. Various students have diverse learning styles, so the ideal approach to furnishing them with useful learning resources is sight and sound. You may utilize YouTube and assist visual students with videos. Also, give a digital podcast to students who learn better with sound and intuitive games for students who do better through gamification of learning.

But, if you wish to get intuitive and precise feedback, you should make video updates and video presentations on your course. These videos may include:

- Discussions regarding next week's assignments and their specific subtleties. Additionally, best practices and questions from students regarding different assignments.

- Discussions about the lessons of the past week or any information which needs any update or support.

- More information to the primary content: some industry-based tips and hacks.

- You could make on-the-spot learning through VoiceThread, for your students to collaborate with you and each other during interpretation.

All of this will help in keeping your audiovisual course fascinating, and it will also help in improving your students' understanding.

Foster Collaborative Learning

This teaching strategy is a brilliant method to increase the motivation of students to learn. It happens through group learning. In this teaching strategy, a small group of students collaborates on a specific project or task.

Henceforth, the responsibility for and teaching is shared by the group of students. It gives your students substantially more chances to actively take part in their learning, in asking questions, and in evaluating one another. Furthermore, your students will show signs of improvement and willingness to share; they will talk about their thoughts directly and apply what they have learned.

If you design the exercises carefully, you can help your students learn the skills they need to work as a team effectively. These organized conversations additionally help to avoid arguments and fights.

Another way to avoid these contentions is to encourage your students to speak with one another and to have meaningful conversations. Also, create a classroom that would promote a safe platform for meaningful and attentive conversations—including questions to offer ascent to result-oriented arguments.

Engage Them in Decision Making

Nothing could be more empowering than permitting an individual to become a part of critical decision-making processes. While this is a typical practice in the business world to enable workers to feel drawn in, the same practice can also build stronger connections with your online students. So, let your students partake in the decision-making process of the class. For example, allow them to pick the projects which they are going to do or the specific points which you will examine in a personal essay. The most important thing is that you make them feel they are a real part of the online teaching course.

Support Intelligent Communication

The most direct way to promote connection is to support intelligent communication. It may include texting or live chats.

Encourage your students to benefit as much as possible from whatever form of intelligent conversations you all decide on, whether it is moderated conversations or off and on conversations. Encourage them to leverage on this opportunity to connect you and their schoolmates, concerning their project conversations or group projects.

Define Your Student Reward System

Prizes are a great way to keep your students motivated. It causes them to be more interested in the course, helping them to focus on learning. Since individuals acknowledge rewards, many teachers benefit as much as possible from remunerations systems to get the attention of their students. These prizes can be given at the end of projects or group exercises.

Another approach to connect with your students is to consider their suggestions when choosing the prize. An award for finishing the course of action will persuade your students to invest tremendous energy in learning, and they will consistently stay connected with you and focused on the course's goals.

As an online instructor, all your students need to have the ideal learning involvement with your courses. A personal connection between you and a student can influence their levels of commitment and information retention and success. Creating opportunities for personalized communication and building a

connection, while both essential parts of online teaching, are not the same. Personalized communication is only one way to build positive connections with your online students.

MOTIVATE STUDENTS TO TAKE ZOOM CLASS LESSONS

Inspiration is, in all actuality, one of the essential mainstays of a fruitful classroom. As a mentor, you're never going to achieve your objective without moving your understudies. Inspiration is certifiably not an entangled idea, and it's anything but a troublesome activity to spur the understudies. We live our lives with satisfaction and joy, with torment and distress, since we are motivated to push ahead. Better believe it, regularly being disregarded and disappointed in our lives, we keep away from our expectation of pushing ahead. Yet, when the human instinct is empowered, we begin to reconsider pushing ahead. Similarly, as a rule, without being animated, the understudy loses would like to learn. That is the reason understudies should be propelled.

An educator can't be a decent instructor, except if he realizes how to move a student. An astounding teacher is an individual who knows the realities and strategies of how to make a functioning classroom, where the understudy can partake excitedly. As a general rule, without inspiring your understudies, you won't have the option to satisfy your sole duty.

Probably the best thoughts for empowering the understudies in the school are talked about underneath. As a general rule, these tips on persuading your understudies can assist you in making your classroom progressively beneficial and innovative.

Guarantee Anxiety-Free Classroom

What do you know? Dread additionally represses learning results. Along these lines, never try to force fear by authorizing disciplines in your classroom. I have discovered that a few of us, the educators, are executing additional assignments as a discipline, because physical controls don't happen in showing today, as in the old and traditional period. Likewise, negative comments regularly offer ascent to fear among understudies in the classroom. The dread in the classroom, regardless of whether it's for revenge or compromising remarks, will never motivate the students. In all actuality, dread is a hindrance to taking an interest effectively in the learning meeting. The understudy ought to never look to take a functioning part in the classroom. That is the reason each educator ought to keep up a dread free class to rouse the understudies. Along these lines, they never offer negative expressions and troubling errands as disciplines.

Promote Their Ideas and Decisions

To advance innovative learning in the homeroom. Even though it offers assignments and coursework, giving them their opportunity to pick the subject all alone, your understudies will be motivated. You know, all things considered, that individuals need appreciation. Truly, thankfulness changes a lot of understudies 'lives. Your understudies can't hold on to partake in your next talk. What's more, if you appreciate new thoughts, several incredible thoughts will be presented to different understudies in your homeroom. So consistently welcome new plans to motivate your understudies.

Explain the Objective

Each understudy enjoys clear guidelines. Explain every objective and target objective to be cultivated toward the start of the course. Remember to refer to the impediments they may look during the meeting. Examine potential cures about the difficulties they may confront. They will, subsequently, be propelled to address more issues, which will make the subject progressively available. Accordingly, you will find that your homeroom has become fruitful because your understudies are empowered.

"As an instructor, you are setting up a nation, another world that will come before long guideline you and the earth."

Improve the Environment of the Classroom

Don't generally plunk down to talk about the exercise. Move next to the students and consider the experience. Keep them out of your group once in a while. Instruct them to visit the library now and again for investigation purposes. The move in the classroom condition animates the energy of the learning cerebrum, which is essential for inspiration.

Be a Good Listener

Listen cautiously to what your understudy needs to state. Value their feelings and conclusions. Find a way to take care of the issues they talk about. Be an incredible audience, fellow. They're going to begin adoring you when you hear them out with legitimate consideration. You will win their certainty, hence. Presently, is it difficult to move them? You need to hear them out first.

Share Their Experience

Not all understudies can share their involvement with the course of the class. Understanding books will involve some of them. However, as sure understudies examine their exercises related mastery, others might be motivated to take an interest effectively. Set up the exercise in such a compelling way that different kinds of students can connect virtually to share exercises. In this circumstance, different understudies are regularly propelled to share their encounters. You can, subsequently, guarantee that the classroom is significant.

Positive Competition

The helpful rivalry is, fundamentally, a valuable system in the school. Guarantee the contention is productive. A decent contention in bunch work propels students hugely. We are additionally arranged to complete network work, which will likewise carry significant advantages to their expert life. There is no uncertainty that good rivalry sparkles energy among the understudies in the classroom.

Know your Student Well

You have to realize your understudies well. You ought to likewise know their inclinations, their aversions, their viability, and their absence of execution. At the point when your understudies understand that you realize them well, they will start to like you and reveal their hindrances. It would be simpler for you to motivate your understudies correctly. You won't have the option to energize them since you realize them well.

Support Them and Give Them Responsibility

Give them the obligation of the understudies. Allot them a class venture. They're going to work with assurance without a doubt. In such a circumstance, singular understudies may likewise need to satisfy their commitments. At the point when you give them obligations, trust inside themselves will develop, and they will start to feel that they are significant because they get an incentive from you. They would then be propelled to connect more in the classroom. At the point when you confide in them, they will consistently confide in you consequently.

Show Your Enthusiasm

To convey your excitement in the classroom during a talk while meeting your obligations. Offer your energy about their extraordinary achievement. Once more, it shows a romantic premium when each student presents another thought. Your demeanour of excitement will empower them.

Hold Your Record

Compose a report for you. Record each achievement of your understudy. On the off chance that you locate that a particular understudy is changing, address the understudy about change. Show the understudy the record. Rewards and bolster the understudy before the classroom. Indeed, even offer the progressions with your companions, on the off chance that an understudy finds that you're dealing with the understudy. At the same time, your address from your record, and the understudy is enlivened.

Valuable Feedback

On the off chance that an understudy isn't progressing nicely, incorporate positive input. At the point when vital, offer another opportunity. Be a companion and look to comprehend the instance of such an awful outcome. Urge the understudy to rouse him/her to improve rapidly next time as he/she didn't see how to do well in this subject with legitimate information and procedure. Alright, guess what? Your valuable surveys will change many lives. Take a gander best case scenario understudies in your school; you will get many good characteristics. Advise them regarding the delightful conditions they have. As a general rule, esteem them, which will rouse them altogether consequently.

Real-life Situation In the classroom

Relate your exercise plan to an actual situation. Make the exercise charming with the fun of the game. Reveal to it an astounding story with a blend of amusingness. The perusing along these lines makes it feasible for the understudy to react to their understanding. Let them likewise apply the exercise to their understanding. Just track it precisely. In actuality, when you're managing your perusing, in actuality, situations, understudies are urged to learn and go to your group.

Bottom line

An educator must guarantee that the classroom is dynamic. Educators ought not to say that they can simply enter and leave the homeroom with 'Great Stories' without giving a practical class. Through rousing your understudies, you can make the best classroom you're anticipating. Like an educator, you are setting up a nation, another world that will come before long principle you and the planet.

Communicate with Your Parents and Guardians

Utilize the homeroom to keep the guardians and gatekeepers on the up and up. You should welcome guardians to pursue an ordinary or week by week email overview of what's happening in their kids' schools. Messages contain the pending or incomplete work of an understudy, just as updates and questions you post in the class stream.

Allotting Assignments to a Group of Students

Instructors may designate work and post-declarations to singular understudies or a gathering of understudies in a class. This usefulness encourages instructors to recognize guidance as required, just as to advance community-oriented gathering work.

Utilizing the Classroom Mobile App Annotations

Understudies and instructors can utilize the Mobile Classroom on Android, iOS, and Chrome cell phones. You can give a contribution to constant by explaining the understudy's work in the application. Understudies may likewise record their assignments to pass on a thought or idea all the more without any problem.

Explore the Integration of Classroom with Other Resources

Google Classroom utilizes an API to connect and trade information with an assortment of your preferred gadgets. Many utilizations and sites are fused, similar to Pear Deck, Actively Read, Newsela, and many, some more.

CONCLUSION

Whether you feel like meeting your friends and collectively having a glass of wine or attending formal meetings and company conferences, Zoom has got you covered. With the devastating pandemic that affects millions of people worldwide, it is becoming strenuous for everyone to keep their minds sane.

If you plan to open a business as soon as the economy becomes more stable, consider video conferencing services such as Zoom as a crucial part of your working conditions. It can not only save you money but also improve productivity, eventually resulting in a decreased turnover and more profits. If you are already running a business, try to incorporate video calls into your regime. If you are a current employee of a company, you can suggest this solution to your boss.

Zoom is providing everything you need for sensational video conferencing at all price ranges. The quality of the video you get is excellent, and the audio is coming through too. You can share multiple screens and annotate projects using whiteboard functions. Zoom also lets you connect to any device that suits you – including your smartphone.

Perhaps Zoom's most significant benefit is how accessible that technology is. Setting up a Zoom Meeting is as easy as clicking on an invitation connection to start the app or asking users to install the GUI. There is no need for any mass-provisioning solutions, and the interface on both mobile and desktop devices is lightweight and straightforward.

Zoom also offers super-fast functionality, with audio and video of high quality at every price point.

The free edition of Zoom equips you with the essential resources available to connect remotely with others. Quality is optimum with this method, even for its users who are not paying. It leans more to the budget-friendly side, relative to other applications of its kind— no need to think twice as Zoom is a bang for the buck.

It is one good video conferencing software despite a few hiccups with Zoom. Its ability to provide high-definition audio and video quality is outstanding, even though it needs a stronger link to the internet. The benefits overall outweigh the drawbacks, and Zoom is worth it.

Zoom is a great way to get everyone together at the same time. You can host a meeting and chat over a glass of wine, organize a game for everyone to play, or create a quiz. The possibilities are endless.

Being a pro at hosting a video conference is essential. But what's also essential is leading the virtual meeting, especially if you are the host or team leader. However, as a participant, you should also actively participate and make the most out of your presence. Now that you have learned all the features that are available in Zoom, you are trained to use this service with expertise.

To sum it up, Zoom offers excellent support, basic and advanced features that enhance a successful video conference, impressive host and participant controls, thorough engagement, and, now, reliable security, making it a complete package.

With Zoom, you can thoroughly practice social distancing while achieving your daily meeting objectives, all virtually. And, as you have seen, this platform is straightforward and effortless to use. With multiple features and an efficient free plan, you are just a click away from downloading and using this outstanding service that will connect you to the world from the comfort of your home. So, whether it's a Pictionary game with your loved ones or an important business meeting, Zoom will assist you through it.

Have fun video conferencing!

GOOGLE CLASSROOM

The Complete Guide for Teachers to Improve the Quality of your Lessons and Motivate your Students

INTRODUCTION

Google Classroom is a web service developed by Google for teachers and schools to make assignments paperless and streamlining the file-sharing system between students and teachers. This uses the whole Google ecosystem, like Google documents, slides and sheets for writing and presenting, the Gmail communication system. For planning, you use Google calendar. Students can participate in the lessons their teachers created using a private code or are automatically imported from the domain. Each class is separated based on folders in the disc, students can put work in it, and teachers can rate it. It's essentially like putting your entire classroom on a computer, and it helps streamline education as well as communication between teachers and students.

The coolest thing is that if you don't want to talk on a computer or use a computer, there are mobile apps for both Android and Apple devices that allow students to do assignments on their device, even post photos, share different apps and files, and also access to information on their devices both online and offline. Even with this, teachers can contact and speak to students, track how a student is doing. Once they have been assessed, teachers can go back and add comments to their work to ensure students receive the best education possible.

In essence, this has made teaching much more productive, it also allows teachers to manage the courses out there, and everything is in one place, making for more meaningful collaboration between both parties and ensuring students get the help they need when the going gets tough.

The system allows more administrative tasks to be performed effectively. Because of the G-suite for education, it makes tasks that are otherwise boring much faster. It works wherever you are, teacher or student, be it from a computer, any mobile device or whatever, and it gives teachers access to the assignments out there, the course materials they need and all the feedback in a great place.

The coolest part about this is that it's free. It's free for schools that have signed up for G Suite for Education, and as with all tools, the classroom meets one of the highest standards out there, and it's a super fun system, it's free and works better than most free software out there.

Another big advantage of this is that I don't allow feedback to return to the student immediately. Teachers can monitor a student's progress and let them know how they are doing. More attention can be paid to ensure that the student gets it, which is what many students want. The nice thing about this is how integrated this is for the workplace for students, and teachers will be able to help in a much timelier manner. Also, it ensures a more personal construction and students can also learn more subjects.

For teachers and students, it saves them time, effort and paper and teachers can create a better environment for assignments and quizzes, and you can always talk to parents and caregivers. You can also copy and modify commands to each other and also manage multiple classes, which is great if you want to master this type of system. It's great for both students and teachers. It creates a collaborative system that in turn will create a better and more immersive system than you thought possible.

Many praises Google Drive for the accessibility of the devices, the use of Google Drive and the ability to work paperless. But it does have the downside that there is little support for third-party services, although that changes, the lack of automatic quizzes and also the lack of live chats that teachers can use for feedback, but it is clear that Google wants to update, so we will may see these changes sooner than ever.

WHAT IS GOOGLE CLASSROOM

In 2014, Google For Education arrived in Brazil promising to bring a whole new perspective on the integration between technology and education. The well-known multinational's proposal is to offer resources to institutions, teachers and students to streamline the teaching-learning process and update educational practices.

G Suite for Education, for example, is available for free and integrates access to institutional email, unlimited storage on Google Drive, Calendar, Google Sheets, Forms and Slides. Another important Google For Education tool is Google Classroom. This online classroom mirror provides more exchange between students and faculty.

This application is a clear example that technology does not separate, but rather when it is well used.

Google Classroom is a management, organization and collaboration tool that makes learning much more productive. Through the platform it is possible to send papers, receive grades, answer questions with teachers and fellow students and much more.

The application's practical interface allows even those who are not very familiar with other technological resources to use it without difficulty. The goal is to make the dynamics of the classes more attractive and, at the same time, more accessible.

Digital Classroom in Practice

But how does it all work, in practical terms? Each student at the institution must register using a specific institutional email for this purpose, which is made available by the institution. Afterwards, the teacher is responsible for connecting all of his students in an online class through the Classroom.

From there, the infinite possibilities of the application will be available, which can and should be used. For the teacher, the tool helps in the management of classes and the ease in dealing with administrative issues, checking grades, passing on announcements and inserting evaluations in the system.

Students also benefit from the tool, making it possible to send jobs and activities much more easily. But the interaction provided by Classroom goes far beyond that and can "save" the undergraduate experience for students.

The lack of updating of teaching methods and individualized monitoring of students are considered two of the main reasons that lead to school dropout in higher education. According to research published in 2007 by the Journal of College Student Retention, innovations in the teaching process and greater communication between teachers and students are fundamental stimuli that lead to the conclusion of the course.

This is the main proposal of the tool. Can be used at any time, it promotes instant communication and serves almost as an educational, social network.

Class members can post links, comments and ask questions, having the opportunity to project their voice without limited time and space, which happens in a conventional classroom.

Teachers can also monitor each student's progress in activities, checking where they need the most support and intervention. There is still space for the assessment to be made in detail, as the digital medium guarantees this flexibility.

Online and Offline

In the case of a distance learning college, constant communication and interaction are fundamental. They even define the quality of the course offered. As distance education courses do not have the presence factor, they need to abuse all available technology to stimulate learning.

The Classroom guarantees fluidity in logistics and a feeling of closeness to the teacher, important requirements so that the student does not feel that he is alone in this journey.

For face-to-face graduation, the new dynamic makes classes more stimulating encourages the participation of all students and still allows for a much more active learning process.

There is still the possibility to connect Classroom with other applications and enhance its functionality. Tools like Classcraft and Quizizz turn regular activities into missions or quizzes, making any job much more fun, without losing focus or quality.

Continue our section on Google tools for a simple dynamic and inclusive teaching.

Google offers free tools that are useful for both teachers and students.

No more long training courses for external management that need constant updates and are difficult to use or superfluous in everyday life.

GOOGLE CLASSROOM AND CORONAVIRUS

In light of the COVID-19 emergency, Google made another website, Teach from Home, specifically intended to assist teachers with acclimating to online courses. The site offers instructional exercises that assist teachers with picking up capability with different G Suite teaching apparatuses. The accompanying tips are planned as an enhancement, in light of numerous long stretches of teaching with online devices.

1. Google Classroom underpins sequenced learning for anybody

Particularly during a period of remote-just work, Google Classroom alongside G Suite applications can bolster learning requirements for a wide range of associations. Any association that utilizes G Suite may utilize Google Classroom: It's not restricted to schools. Classroom makes a practical alternative to enable a teacher to direct any gathering of individuals through an organized arrangement of themes and assignments. While a teacher will often utilize the Classroom with a lot of students, a similar framework can be utilized for proficient improvement endeavor's also.

2. Get setting

Try to comprehend understudy setting before you attempt to pass on content. Students might be managing difficulties not normally present in a school classroom, remembering offspring of different ages for the family unit, grown-ups who may likewise be home, just as a physical situation not really intended to help to learn. To the degree conceivable, set aside some effort to ensure you comprehend the specific situation and conditions of every one of your students.

3. Empower disconnected work

Alter assignments to permit students to work disconnected since only one out of every odd understudy will approach a web association at home. Seat Research examines show that "15% of U.S. family units with young kids don't have a fast web association at home."

Permit access to materials that might be downloaded, rather than spilt. For instance, you may record a video (e.g., with Hangouts Meet) then transfer it to Google Classroom, rather than connecting to a video on YouTube. Likewise, you may give an article you need students to peruse as a PDF or Google Doc, as opposed to a web connection.

If you intend to teach with an especially long book, investigate an EPUB form, which gives the peruser more command over textual styles, text dimension and line separating. An understudy may download and store things including a video document, a PDF, or Google Docs, Sheets, or Slides to Google Drive for disconnected access.

4. Verify that a task should be possible on a cell phone

Preferably, you additionally would check to verify that every task can be finished on an Android telephone, iPhone, or in Chrome on a PC. For instance, most assignments that require the utilization of Google Docs, Sheets, or Slides should function admirably, since those applications function admirably in a program, yet in addition, are accessible to introduce on Android and iOS gadgets.

Presently, the highlights of Docs, Sheets, and Slides differ somewhat by stage. For instance, support differs for additional items (in Docs, Sheets, and Slides), drop-down records (in Google Sheets), and embedded sound or video documents (in Google Slides). Only one out of every odd component works the very same route in each G Suite application on Android, iOS, or Chrome on the web, so it assists with testing new assignments and undertakings.

If you don't approach test your task on the three stages (i.e., Android, iOS, Chrome), contact your school's technical support group. An all-around run IT bolster office will probably have the option to plan time to assist you with verifying that a task can be finished on every stage.

Note: Even if your association gives a gadget to students, I urge you to make unbiased stage assignments so as to augment the opportunities for students to finish an errand, paying little heed to the gadget. Make sure to check assignments for any outsider applications you use, also.

BENEFITS FOR TEACHER

Google Classroom gives the various unmistakable advantage to teachers, but at the same time, it's significant to college students and even designers.

As of late, paperless classrooms have gotten more typical than any other time in recent memory. Indeed, even in rustic territories and at universities, students currently complete most of their work on the web. This change spares a cost for the earth by reducing paper use, and it's likewise helpful for students, particularly the individuals who probably won't approach a real classroom, however go virtually.

Google Classroom was released in the late spring of 2014 and is currently utilized in classrooms around the US. There are numerous advantages to using this free tool.

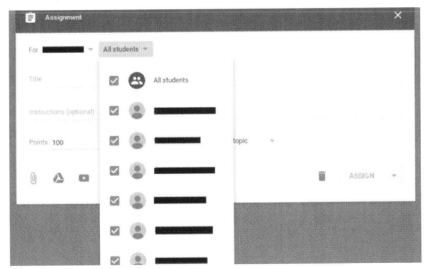

Communication and Collaborate

The in-built tool makes speaking with students and guardians a breeze. Teachers and students can send messages, post to the stream, send private remarks on assignments, and give criticism on work. Teachers have full authority over student remarks and posts. They can likewise speak with guardians through individual messages or through Classroom email announcements which incorporate class declarations and due dates.

The classroom offers a few different ways for students to work together. Teachers can encourage online conversations among students and create group work inside the Classroom. What's more, students can work together on Google Docs, which have been shared by the teacher.

Coordinate It with Other Google Items

Google Classroom likewise coordinates effectively with Google Docs, Sheets, and Slides. For schools on a limited financial plan, offering a platform that matches up with other free tools gives an approach to schools and students to come into the twentieth century without spending a fortune on costly classroom programming.

Teachers give assignments, and students consider those to be a task. When the work is done, the student confirms it. An organized arrangement of steps for task culmination keeps everybody composed and stays away from disarray about which tasks are expected.

Engagement and Differentiation

Most digital natives are OK with innovation and will be increasingly well-suited to take proprietorship in their learning through the utilization of innovation. The classroom offers various approaches to make learning intuitive and synergistic. It offers teachers the capacity to separate assignments, incorporate videos and site pages into videos, and make synergistic gathering assignments.

Through Classroom, teachers are effectively ready to separate instruction for students. Allocating exercises to the entire class, singular students, or gatherings of students makes only a couple of basic steps while making a task on the Classwork page.

Feedback and Data Analysis

Giving significant input to students is an important piece of all learning. Inside the reviewing tool of the Classroom, teachers can send input to every student on assignments. The capacity to make a remark bank for some time later is additionally accessible inside the reviewing apparatus. What's more, the Classroom portable application permits clients to clarify work.

To make learning important, teachers ought to break down information from evaluations to guarantee students understand learning objectives. Information from evaluations can undoubtedly be sent out into Sheets for arranging and investigation.

Exploit a Simple to-Utilize tool

Google Classroom offers a profoundly natural and overly simple-to-learn interface. The platform takes you through each progression of the procedure. At the point when you land on the main page of your classroom, you'll be welcome to "communicate with your group here." You can make announcements and schedule them to go out individually. You can likewise react to any student notes. The interface is plain as well, which implies there's no learning curve to utilizing the product.

ADVANTAGES AND LIMITATIONS OF GOOGLE CLASSROOM

Advantages of Google Classroom

5. Any device

If you are not a regular user of Google, using Google Classroom is one piece of cake. Aside from being provided via the Chrome browser, it can also be used from all laptops, cell phones, and tablets. Teachers may add as many learners as they want. They can create Google Documents to handle assignments and updates, upload YouTube videos, add links, or download files from Google Drive very easily. It will be equally simple for learners to log in and collect and turn in assignments.

6. Clean interface, and user-friendly

Google Classroom invites you while remaining loyal to clean Google layout standards, in an atmosphere where even minute detail about the design is simple, intuitive, and user-friendly. It goes undoubtedly with the saying that users at Google will feel right at home.

7. An excellent device to comment on

For a variety of online courses, the learners may comment on specific locations inside images. Teachers can also create URLs for new comments and use them for further discussion online. This has been shown frequently that technology engages the students. Google Classroom can help students get involved in the learning process and remain active. For example, if teachers have students answering questions in the Classroom, other students will comment on those answers and expand thought for both students.

8. It is for everyone

Educators can also enter Google Classroom as learners, which mean Google Classroom can be set up for you and your co-teachers. You may use it for faculty meetings, exchanging knowledge, or professional development.

9. Language and competencies

When the teacher who produces the class or group of students shares content, teachers may take charge of the language levels and keep them related to their learner community, using language at all levels. Teachers can slowly develop the learning environment and distribute the course materials at their classes' speed, depending on the subject requirements and group profile. The choice of which students they are inviting to specific categories enables teachers to delegate work based on their students' particular learning needs. Teachers can build courses of up to 1000 students and 20 teachers, allowing teaching by a team where appropriate.

10. Content of language learning

A handy feature of Google classroom is that it helps students go through their work once they've submitted it. Teachers will get updates about the students' reworks or feedback on something they find difficult. This ensures they can give the students who need it, individual attention, and give them more opportunities to show their learning, operating at the right speed. Teachers can easily discern knowledge by determining which students may need extra help, who might want to work with response grids of model responses.

The Google Translate plugin for the Classroom is also available to English language teachers.

11. Exposure to an online world

A lot of colleges today expect students to take at least one online class during their degree research. If one gets a Master's degree in education, some of their online coursework might be eligible. Sadly, many of the students never had any online education experience. At a young age, teachers should make sure that their students have as much exposure to the online world as possible. Google Classroom is a simple way for students to assist with this change because it's super user-friendly, making it a perfect technology intro.

12. Differentiation

Google Classroom is an ideal resource for differentiation, as teachers can set up several different classrooms. If teachers focus on a topic in the Classroom and have groups that focus on two different levels, they can simply build two different classes. This means they can reach out to those who struggle with their kind of job without making them feel bad or dumb.

This can help teachers offer assignments on a more individual basis and reach out to some students. They can even break people into groups where teachers think they can work the best together. Google Classroom is a perfect, versatile way to make sure every student gets what they need, and as instructors see fit, they can quickly delete and recreate classes.

13. Saves time and cost

Students lose out on all of the 'hidden' costs of studying at an institution by taking online courses with Google Classroom. This includes travel costs (which in some cases are very high), the costs of printing out assignments, and so on, and the stationary and notebook costs.

Although it is difficult to determine how high these costs would be before the students enrol in a course, some important considerations should be considered. More specifically, how far a student would drive to an educational institution every day (and how much parking fees if they're commuting by car). If that turns out to be a significant number, they could save money by taking online courses.

Most students find that taking Google classes saves them a lot of time since they work from home-no time is spent on regular commuting. They can even take on a part-time job if they have any spare time to earn while studying. This is perfect for those looking to maintain some kind of stable income while at the same time acquiring additional qualifications through Google Classroom.

Limitations of Google Classroom

1. Complex account management

Google Classroom doesn't enable multi-domain access. You can't sign in to access your personal Gmail; you need to sign in to Google Apps for Education. Consequently, if you already have your own Google ID, managing Google Accounts can be challenging. For example, if your Gmail contains a Google document or a picture and you want to share it in the Google Classroom, you need to save it separately on your device's hard drive, log out, and then log in with your Google Classroom account again. Pretty much trouble.

2. Too much 'Googlish.'

Google users can get confused for the first time, as there are several buttons with icons that are only familiar to Google users.

Also, despite improved collaboration between Google and YouTube, which dramatically helps with video sharing, support for other standard tools is not built-in. You can find it annoying that you need to convert a primary Word document to a Google Doc to work with. In the Google Classroom environment, you'll only find yourself relaxed as long as the resources you're using fit with Google services.

3. Problems editing

When you create an assignment and send it to the learners, the learners become the document's "owners" and can edit it. This means they can erase any part of the assignment they choose, which may create problems, even if it happens unintentionally. Also, after you edit a post, students don't get a notification.

Also, there is no direct video recording option. It would be helpful to quickly and directly record voice and video messages into the Classroom at Google. Users can record the videos outside the Classroom, and then upload them as an attachment.

4. Sharing work with learners

Learners cannot share their work with their classmates unless they become "owners" of a document, and even then, they will have to accept sharing options, which will create a rift if they want to share a report with their 50 + classmates say.

5. Limited integration

Google has restricted integration options and still needs to expand these options.

6. Updates are not automated

Event feed does not automatically update, so learners have to check and regularly refresh to avoid missing important announcements.

There are both advantages and limitations of Google Classroom. Nevertheless, benefits certainly outweigh the drawbacks. Despite safeguards in place to prevent the spread of the virus, and the school year potentially cancelled for thousands of students, Google Classroom is an integrating spot, considering the current state of affairs. Its usage is safe. Educators can post in an ad-hoc fashion all the essential materials, assignments, and quizzes. The software may assist private tutors, as well as home-school parents.

BENEFITS FOR THE STUDENTS

Permit Students to Interface with Different Students

One component of Google Classroom is making assignments, for example, questions. You can set up what number of focuses an inquiry is worth and even permit students to associate with each other. A simple to-get to gathering encourages collaboration, even in an online environment, and empowers students to gain from each other.

Notwithstanding the students interfacing with each other, the teacher can associate with singular students and even with guardians through email, presents on a stream, private remarks and criticism. You can likewise make a class declaration that applies to all the students enlisted.

Learn to Use an Online Classroom Platform

Several universities have recently used a combination of physical appearance and online classroom environments. This is a huge benefit as using Google Classroom helps you to experience an online environment as either as a teacher or a student.

As a teacher, you can also login in as a student and see out how the platform works so that you can know how to guide any confused students. This is a new level of learning, as the world increasing in technology, expects even more online courses, even for topics such as web designing, where students can now learn a lesson online and upload his or her work via a whiteboard or even as an attachment.

Q Search Drive

My Drive ▾

Name ↓   Owner

🗂 Classroom   me

Accessibility and Time Saver

Google Classroom can be gotten from any PC employing Google Chrome or from any cell phone. All files transferred by teachers and students are uploaded in a Classroom folder on Google Drive. Clients can get to the Classroom whenever, anyplace. Students no longer need to stress over smashed PCs or hungry mutts.

Google Classroom is a huge time saver. With all the different resources compressed in one place, which gives you the ability to access the Classroom anywhere, there will be more free-time for teachers to complete any other tasks. Since everyone can access the Classroom from a mobile device, teachers and students can participate through their phones or tablets.

Then for students, all their resources for a class can be found in one single place. So, there's no need to find a book, grab a notebook, rush to the classroom for a lecture, or to print out an essay. Instead, the class lessons can be viewed online, reply to questions, and even submit work all in one place. The interface stays neat and organized, so there will be no need wasting time looking for that lost classroom materials.

For teachers, all of the students, information, submissions, and grades are in one convenient location.

Stops the Excuses

A few students appear to have an excuse for not turning in their work ceaselessly. You've heard the old "the dog ate my schoolwork" answer, yet a few students take reasons to another level. With an advanced classroom, work is relegated and submitted web-based, which means it can't be "lost." Online platforms additionally permit guardians to keep steady over what their student finished what despite everything needs wrapping up.

A few schools are likewise using web-based learning on snow days as opposed to compelling students to make up scratch-offs because of extraordinary climate. Never again is spring break cut into or school in meeting for seven days after it ought to have finished. Rather, the school gives access to web-based learning modules so work proceeds even on days when school doesn't.

The Future is here

Google is on the front line of innovation and what individuals look for from online frameworks. An online classroom framework permits schools and individuals who simply need to offer information to others a spot to do as such without going through a great deal of cash. The free efficiency tools likewise give you a spot to keep classes sorted out and store reports.

Google Classroom smoothed out the whole instruction process by dispensing with the need to print and duplicate papers and physically enter grades into an evaluation book. Rather, everything is done carefully, sparing time, and exertion. Teachers additionally save time and can concentrate on individualized learning.

HOW TO SET UP GOOGLE CLASSROOM

Logging in With Google Classroom

Step 1

Go to class.google.com

Step 2

Sign in with your school Google account details

Step 3

Scroll down and select "Teacher."

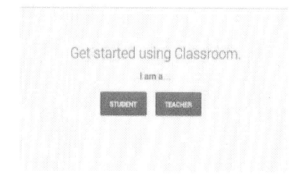

Step 4

Build your first class by clicking "+" Adding class

<u>Adding A Class</u>

Step 1

Sign in to Classroom using your swcsd.us email address

Step 2

Click at the top of the page and click create class

Step 3

Enter the class name in the first text box

Create a class

Class name

Section

CANCEL   CREATE

Step 4

Enter a short description in the second text box, such as section, grade level, or class time

Create a class

Technology Applications

Section

CANCEL   CREATE

Step 5

Click "Create"

Create a class

Technology Applications

Quarter 1 Period 2

CANCEL   CREATE

Applying A Theme

Step 1

Locate "change class theme" on the header (top right-hand corner)

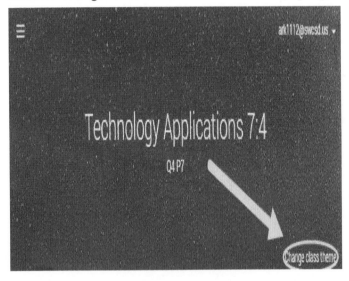

Step 2

Select a theme you like from the gallery by clicking on it.

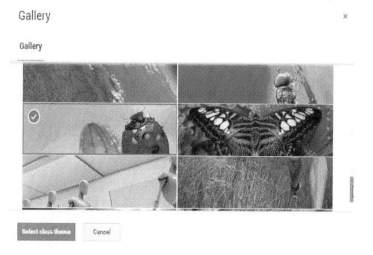

Step 3

Click "Select class theme"

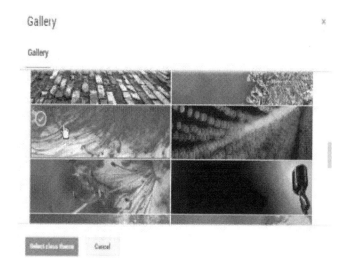

Setting Notifications

Step 1

Click the three bars in the top left-hand corner, scroll to the bottom and click "Settings"

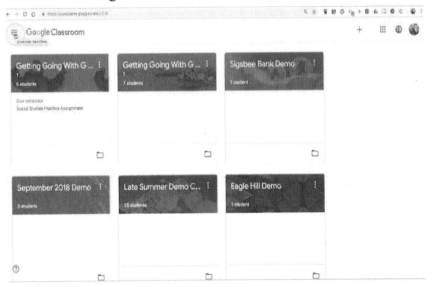

Step 2

Put a checkmark next to the "Send email notifications" if you would like to receive them or deselect if you would no longer like to receive the notifications. You will recently receive notifications any time a student posts or comments on the stream. You do not receive notifications about students turning in assignments.

Will Receive Notification

Will Not Receive Notifications

Step 3

Automatically all the changes will be solved

Student Management

how to get students enrolled in your course and change the settings that affect your students will be tackled. Students are the most crucial part of the school, and having them adequately registered is vital to the success of the school.

Select all

Adding Students by Code

Step 1

A "Class File" is created automatically by Google Classroom and will appear on the left side of your "Path."

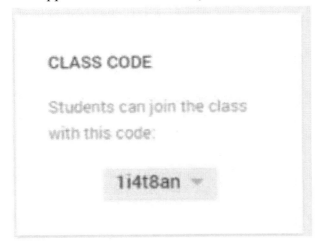

Step 2

Ask students to visit classroom.google.com and from their home page, click "+" in the top right corner, and then "Enter Class" * If this is their first time to log in to classroom.google.com See the tech leader get students to enter their first class.

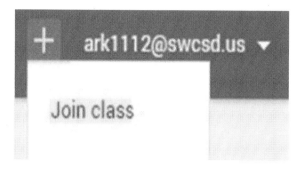

Step 3

Ask students to insert the code you are giving them in the box provided. Students can then pick "Enter."

Enter class code to join.

CANCEL   JOIN

Reset or Disable Class Code

Step 1

Go to your "Source" and find the class code on the left sidebar.

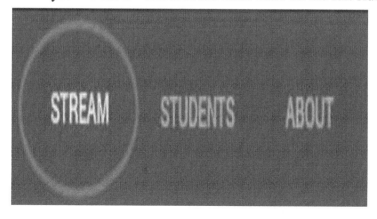

Step 2

Press the drop-down arrow next to the code to update the class code and press "Delete." Google Classroom is going to create a new application for you. You are not in a position to build your system.

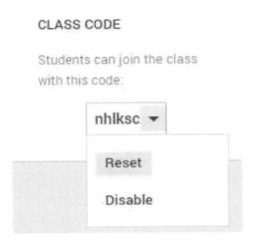

Step 3

To disable the account code (no one would be able to enter your account by default), select the drop-down arrow next to the negligence and press "Disable."

Sorting of Students

Step 1

Pick "STUDENTS" from the top menu bar.

Step 2

Choose "Students" and then select "Sorting by First Name" or "Sorting by Last Name"

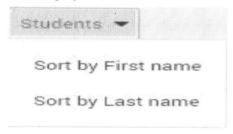

Emailing Students

Step 1

Choose "STUDENTS" on the top navigation screen.

Step 2

Pick students you want to email or press "Select all" button

Step 3

Press "ACTIONS" at the top of the screen and then "Email."

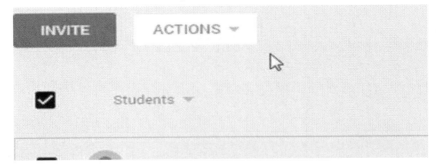

Step 4

You will be sent to your Gmail account, and all selected students will appear in the "BCC" area.

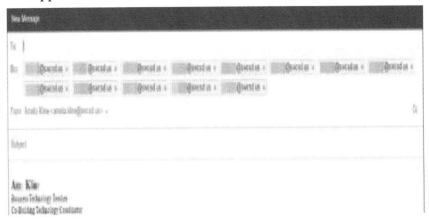

Removing Students from Class

Step 1

Click "STUDENTS" on the top navigation screen

Step 2

Select the student you want to delete by clicking the checkbox next to the student's name.

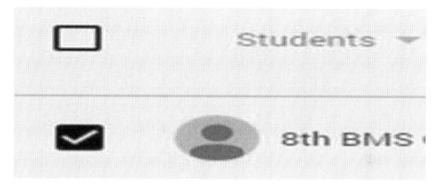

Step 3

Pick "ACTIONS" at the top of the window and then "Delete."

Step 4

In the dialog box, ask if you are sure you want to disable the student.
Click "Delete"

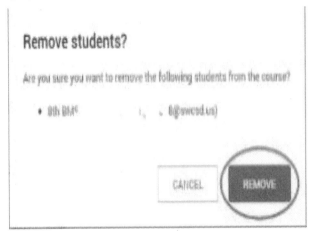

HOW GOOGLE CLASSROOM CAN HELP WITH CLASSROOM INTERACTION

If you want to build a more connected platform for students, you might be considering doing so on the Stream page of Google Classroom. The Stream is a feed within Google Classroom where everybody in the class can find announcements and upcoming assignments, and it is the first thing students see when they log in.

Some teachers use the Stream to set up class discussion boards, where students can connect online by asking questions or commenting on the posts. Such discussion boards will help improve class engagement and give more leverage to students in getting their voices heard (or read) by the teacher. You can use the Stream as a closed social network of sorts with conversations, and it can be a great way to help children practice using all kinds of different digital citizenship skills in a "walled garden" style environment. Google promotes interaction in its classroom application to ensure a more significant outcome.

Engagement through student-teacher interaction

Once a student logs in to complete an assignment, they will make a class comment to which all other class-fellows and the teachers assigned to that class will receive a notification (through email and app notification) that students and teachers will reply to. This can be an enormous opportunity for both the teacher and students because they can answer a question or assist the whole class with a misunderstanding.

A student can also send a private message to the teacher if they want to ask a question without their classmates' prying eyes. After all, the same social problems are evident in the digital world as in the Classroom (How many times did you, as a teacher, have to deal with student social media conflicts?).

The following ways can bring in more significant student-teacher interaction with Google Classrooms.

With Google Classrooms, teachers can:

• Organize, distribute, and compile assignments, materials for the course, and student research online. Teachers are often able to post a task to different classes or to change and repeat assignments year after year. This would bring in some interaction between teachers and their students.

• Communicate about the classwork with the students. They can use the site to post announcements and notes about tasks, and it is easy to see who has finished their job or who has not. They may also check in privately with individual students, answer their questions and give support, as already mentioned in the beginning.

• Offer timely feedback to the students on their assignments and assessments. Google Forms can be used inside Google Classroom to build and exchange quizzes, which are automatically graded as students turn them in. Not only would the teachers spend less time grading, but their students will provide direct feedback on their work.

Engagement through videos

Educators can provide grades or reviews electronically without ever having to deal with paperwork by using open technology. Additionally, all work on the course is saved so that students can revisit it while they are at home. Students can also complete assignments via Google Classroom and communicate with teachers. This two-way communication method makes teaching and learning using the platform more convenient. By incorporating video, it makes engaging students even more comfortable.

Below are some reasons why videos could be helpful in a Google Classroom:

• Video facilitates collaboration and learning: In Google Classroom, multimedia is used by educators to improve the course work. Many are making videos within their class as interactive learning resources. By using video platforms, educators can create video tutorials or lessons, provide student input, use as assignments for students, or capture lectures all with a click of the record button.

• Feasibility in access: By using videos, educators can interact effectively and keep students learning without ever having to waste time in class. The videos are sent home and viewed in flipped or mixed learning scenarios. The student will learn from home, which makes them more interested in the Classroom.

The Classroom is an online application that can be used anywhere. Educators are given access to their videos on multiple devices with an account. They can quickly jump between devices and have access to video recordings.

With the Chromebook apps, educators and students both can record and share their videos. Videos can be stored directly on Google Drive. All files uploaded are stored in a folder in the Classroom. This makes videos easily accessible to teachers as well as students.

• Saves Time: Video is incredible for time-saving. Forget about typing out long assignments or grading documents! With video, educators can film assignments and be able to assign them all in a few minutes. The educators will add a video file with instructions when they make an assignment in a Classroom.

• Encourages teamwork and communication: Video encourages collaboration and strengthens conversations. Google Classroom gives students several ways to work together. Teachers can encourage online student-to-student discussions and create group projects within the tool. Students will hold talks with each other with video and complete tasks as assigned to them. Also, students can collaborate on Google Docs and share their work with teachers easily.

It is an immersive learning environment that is collaborative. By using videos, they can further enrich the experience. With Classroom, teachers can separate assignments, integrate videos and web pages into classes, and create shared group assignments for students.

• Strengthens the student-teacher bond: Video provides a more reliable link with the students. Positive feedback is needed for students to learn. This is a worthy aspect of all learning. So why not do it by video? Recent studies have shown that at a higher level, video mentoring and feedback requires students to communicate with teachers. It gives them a bond that they would otherwise not get in a group environment. Video offers a one-to-one friendship without being face to face.

Google Classroom educators can easily grade assignments. They can give any student personalized feedback. There's also the opportunity to comment on the grading tool. Additionally, the Classroom app in smartphones helps users to annotate research. Google Classroom can save all kinds of grades quickly.

Record the video, go to the screen recorder and press the 'record' button. You need to upload and publish the video when it is finished and provide the students with the link. They can access it from anywhere.

Film and share every instructional video with your students. You can monitor them while they watch the video lecture. You will be able to see if your pupils watched your video. You will also realize when the students started watching exactly, and to what section they kept coming again. Video analytics help you understand what interests or engages your students, which part of the video needs further detail, and where your students lose interest.

Engagement through student-student interaction

Originally, while using the class comment feature initially, teachers did find some sorts of distractions-there was all the usual chatter typical in social media design. However, once the students started using Google Classroom, the teachers began to note a slightly unexpected advantage of the class comment feature. Students began to answer each other's questions. In their online Google classrooms, not all classes or students do this, but the ones who do excel. While teachers need to step in and answer a few questions, students do teach one another for the most part!

The SRS (Student Response System) built into the platform is a prominent new feature. This helps teachers to inject questions into the stream page of the Classroom and start question-driven discussions with students answering each other's answers. Teachers may post a video, photo, or article, for example, and include a question that they want their students to answer. This way, teachers can learn and check in on the progress of their students, which is a fundamental practice. They can do that very quickly with this new functionality, from anywhere at any moment.

To increase interaction among online students, teachers can assign them group projects. Forcing students to work together will add new experiences for the students and contribute to strong collaboration among them. The most efficient way of learning is group learning. This offers students a chance to support their fellow mates and to learn to work together. Teachers should get the students together in small groups to prepare and let them and their team create a video project. They may ask them to take photos, record meetings, and upload and complete the project documents such as pictures or audio files.

However, if the students don't get along or their work styles aren't compatible, it can also backfire. Online, this dynamic can be exacerbated because students work with only a limited understanding of the personalities and activities of their fellow students.

Parental inclusion in Google Classroom

With the Google Classroom App, you can connect parents' email addresses to their kids, which helps parents to monitor their child's home learning closely. Parents, although, cannot see or engage with class feedback, they simply receive an email notification that their child has a home learning assignment, so it is important to have parental buy-in to ensure that students develop and accomplish as much as possible. Google refers to parents and families as "guardians" who may elect to receive summaries of unfinished assignments, upcoming assignments, and other class activity by email.

One way to ensure greater parental involvement in Google Classroom learning experience is to organize the evening meetings for the parents and teachers. Teachers and staff can use Google Classroom as a centralized place to book evening appointments for parent-teacher consultation. All instructors are included in Google Classroom, and they can consider the creation of an appointment sheet much as and when students are given an assignment. In such a form, teachers can book meeting dates with their students, and the school administration would immediately know when the appointment is. This might help make the whole evening coordinated much better and run smoother.

CORRELATIONS BETWEEN GOOGLE CLASSROOM, HOME SCHOOLING, ONLINE LEARNING, VIRTUAL EDUCATION

Let's not say that traditional learning should be stopped. However, online learning is not only a viable alternative, but an excellent alternative. Some teachers and trainers prefer to use a mixed approach: combining both methods to maximize results.

If you are a teacher or trainer, we recommend that you consider the benefits of online learning and how it can make your life much easier without decreasing quality.

Free Google Classroom for students and teachers: how to use the tool to study at home

The platform helps organize activities and allows you to download files, among other things

Studying at home is becoming easier with the help of technology, an example of this are the **Google** tools, which were made available to all students, teachers and entrepreneurs during this stage of confinement created by coronavirus.

The **technology giant** shared a diversity of courses through the internet to feed education in Mexico.

Such is the case of G Suite and **Classroom**, which according to the Secretary of Public Education, Esteban Moctezuma, were created so that both teachers and students could study for free, in such a way that there was no interruption in their learning, in addition to a benefit for entrepreneurs.

Google Classroom was officially created in 2014; However, it took root until this **2020 and gained popularity among students, since they could not attend school classrooms.**

How to use the Classroom tool?

Any person who wants to occupy **Google Classroom** must identify themselves with a **Google or Gmail account** that they must create in order to use said platform.

Then you must enter the internet page classroom.google.com, where you must first check the account with which the interested party is identified, by clicking continue.

Then press the + button located in the upper right where you can **select the class** already created or create a new one. If you write one, the URL address of the class assigned by your teacher will be requested.

Upon entering there are several tabs that will help the student to coordinate and organize their tasks and work.

Files can also be attached **through a link, from the computer, from Google Drive or upload YouTube videos.**

With the tool you can create or select classes. (Photo: Special)

In addition, new participants (students) can be entered and teachers will be able to grade and upload works, allowing remote connection and supervision of students.

What is G Suite?

G Suite is the other Google tool that was designed to control and manage companies with their own domain.

In it you can generate professional email addresses, example your name @ example. com

In April, Google shared one more way to spend time and stay home during this COVID-19 spread period, and offered **classes and courses for small** and medium-sized enterprises (SMEs), so they can develop better learning techniques and overcoming.

The initiative **"grows with Google at home" was aimed at entrepreneurs, business owners, employees, educators, journalists, among others,** who could access some free tools such as Google My Business, which serves to maintain communication with customers.

Through virtual conferences on **YouTube**, the Internet platform offered **three training sessions.**

"The goal of staying connected, improving productivity at work and learning at home, managing businesses remotely and acquiring new **digital skills**, "the company said in a statement.

The virtual courses were some such as: "Free Google tools to help your SME", in which a three-session **course,** with 35 minutes each, **was offered**, aimed at small and medium entrepreneurs, in addition to Google for Education for teachers, through which teachers learned to implement various teaching materials and strategies.

The implementation of other tools such as: Gmail, Hangouts Meet and Google Drive, Chat, Calendar, Docs was recalled. In addition to tips to use them in the best way.

Virtual Education Advantages, fantasies and tips to improve results

You may as of now be persuaded that virtual instruction is a phenomenal decision for learning and giving information. Or on the other hand it might be that you despite everything have your questions about the viability of this sort of instruction and its degree.

What is a reality is that virtual training keeps on picking up prominence? In excess of 6,000,000 students at present take at least one online course; half of colleges offer in any event one online program.

... And these numbers will just keep on developing as the consolidation of new advancements proceeds in this day and age.

In a couple of years, this instructive model will be the standard around the globe.

Given my profession as a pioneer in college advanced change, and in the current setting wherein there are still individuals who are not persuaded about virtual instruction, I share this article where I list the primary advantages, I deny a few fantasies and I offer some great practices to take consider.

Primary preferences of virtual training

In the event that you haven't taken an online course yourself, have you at any point thought about what the experience of realizing for all intents and purposes is truly similar to? In spite of the fact that the internet learning stages utilized may contrast marginally, virtual training offers numerous advantages contrasted with the conventional showing technique, for instance:

• Expanding learning openings: One of the principle advantages of virtual instruction is that it offers a wide assortment of assets to the instructor, from virtual visits, online libraries with curated assets, intuitive assessments, associations with specialists around the globe, and so on. With new advancements, classes can be imaginative and participatory consistently.

• Learn anyplace: you just need an electronic gadget (phone, tablet or PC) to get to consider materials.

• You can pick when to consider: numerous students work; For this explanation, virtual instruction permits them to keep gaining from anyplace and whenever. An investigation asked students for what valid reason do they decide to learn on the web? Most reacted that as a result of the comfort and adaptability offered by the projects. The greater part (59%) of the overviewed students have youngsters, and half revealed that they additionally have an occupation.

• Responsibility and self-sufficiency: making a daily schedule and doing the comparing exercises is a word of wisdom for effectively finishing the projects advertised.

Breaking fantasies to increment instructive reach

In spite of the exponential development of virtual instruction, numerous individuals despite everything think of it as a second-rate sort of training.

I am here to disclose to you that these convictions are a long way from reality, and that online instruction can be as believable, dependable, useful, and viable as conventional training.

Homeschooling and virtual teaching

This virtual teaching style is an interaction between a student and a teacher. The virtual classroom is usually set up through teleconferences. Communication is available in various forms, such as messages, audio and visual.

One-to-one teaching tips

• Get to know your individual students

There are factors to consider when considering one-to-one instruction. Getting to know your individual student is a good start. This allows you to fine-tune your goals and tailor the curriculum to students' skills.

• Be flexible with the subject

Relevance is key when speaking to a person. The more you get to know a person, the more you can determine what motivates him. Use this background to your advantage. Use flexible content when working with individuals, and always let them know their progress and ask for continuous feedback.

• Check and recheck student progress

How do you know if the students have learned or not? Check their learning progress. Curriculum-based monitoring tests are helpful. Other reliable tools include interaction, observation, frequent evaluations and formative assessment. Every interaction has to improve and the progress of the students has to improve.

Let the students speak

The education-oriented strategy has been used by virtual teachers. In the 21st century, practical activities are much better. This makes learning more fun, increases retention, promotes engagement, offers opportunities for criticism, guarantees extra practice, stimulates problem-solving skills and stimulates creativity.

Hands-on experiences also allow your class to build confidence, interact with peers, and become productive individuals.

Live streaming

Another teaching style in the virtual classroom is live streaming. What is it? What makes it different from other educational strategies? How can you integrate live streaming into online teaching? How do you keep your viewer's attention? How do you measure the learning progress of participants?

Live streaming: overview

Live streamed classes have only one-way interaction between a virtual teacher and a student. It is set up as a social media platform. As a main subject, the teacher delivers the content to an unknown audience. Examples included are teleconferences and webinars.

How is live streaming going to change the future of learning?

There was a time when we learned by listening to a boring lecture in a traditional classroom. In this digital age, live streaming has changed the teaching methodology as students can view almost everything related to their learning topics. They can follow the experts in the field, they can communicate with peers around the world, and they can even record their own progress.

Live streaming allows interaction outside of the classroom experience. Teachers and students can have personal interaction. Recorded lessons stimulate collaboration, accessibility, diversity, mobile learning, and access to knowledge and are cost effective.

How can you include live streaming in your education?

Staging is imperative when running live streams

Staging is critical in creating educational live streams; it takes extra effort and time. Clean your background before the cameras come on. Make sure you see everything the audience sees. From there, set up your camera, internet connection and audio.

Scripting is critical

The audio is in perfect condition. The background is clean and unique. What else do you need to prepare? Now write the script to avoid empty air in live streams. But don't rely on the script word for word, just use it as a guideline so you don't sound like a robot. Be confident in your knowledge and familiar with the information you present.

Timing is necessary

Timing is another important factor in creating a live stream. Respect your audience's time. Do not rush, avoid going off topic and delete unused sentences.

How do you keep your viewer's attention?

Giving an English lesson via a live stream is fun and interactive ... for the teacher. But holding the viewer's attention until the end of the live stream is complicated. Use a lively voice and tone when referring to the relevant material. Remember regular productive speech patterns such as appropriate breaks and speed.

How do you measure success?

Since live stream is a one-way interaction, how would you know that your virtual instruction was a success? Your audience's participation is a good sign. You can conduct a survey or encourage students to view more content.

Virtual classroom

A virtual classroom setup is two-way communication between a teacher and a group of students. The public can be distributed geographically or in the same space.

As with traditional instruction, teachers provide instructions, assignments and homework to students in a virtual classroom.

In addition to the facilitator, there are moderators and teachers who assist with administrative and technical tasks. As a virtual teacher you have to act as a team captain, coordinate everyone's activities and facilitate the student's performance.

HOW TO CREATE AND SET CLASSES

Classes are fun to create, we will go over how you create a class, organize and manage the class, and how you can remove classes once they are done. Classes are the most important aspect of this, since it's where everyone will be, and if you know how to put all of this together, you'll be well on your way to a successful result with Google Classroom.

How to Create a Class

Now, once you've logged in it's time to create a class. When you first log in, you'll get the option of either student or teacher. Always make sure that you indicate that you are the teacher, and if you mess up, you need to contact the administrator to reset it. It's super important, because students are limited in their options compared to teachers, and it can be quite frustrating. Now, if you're a student, you simply press the plus button when you get it, to join a class. Teachers need to press on 'create a class'.

Now, if you've already got classes, chances are you'll see some other names there. They'll be displayed on the screen itself, but every time you press the plus button, you'll then be able to add more.

Next, you're given a class dialogue boss. You'll then type in the name, and the section for this. You'll be able to create the class immediately from here.

But if you want to add more to it, you can go to the about tab, choose the title of the course, along with the description of it, the location and even add materials here. You do need to have a name for the class itself, since this is how students will find the class when they open it up. If you have classes with multiple names on it, you'll definitely want to specify, either via time or day, especially if you've got a lot of sections. The section field is how you do this, and you can create a subject as well, based on the list of subjects they provide for you.

Some teachers like to make these very descriptive, and you should ideally add as much information as you feel is needed for it. But do remember to make sure it isn't some wall of text that students will read and get confused with. As a teacher, you should make sure you do this in a way that students will get the information easily, and that they'll be able to delineate each class. It's also important to make it easy for your own benefit.

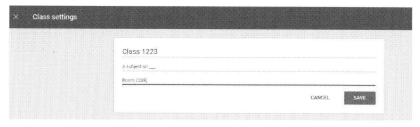

How to Manage a Class

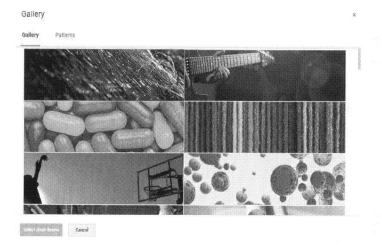

First thing that you can do when changing the class and managing it, is give it a theme. One thing you'll notice is that you don't have students in there as soon as it's created so that you can have a bit of fun with it. One way to do this is, on the right side near the header of the general class, you can change the class theme. You can use the themes that are provided. Some photos of classes themselves are good options, and you can use different templates for each one so that you know exactly what theme you're using, because they can sometimes be a bit complicated.

How to Remove, Delete and View a Class

When using Google Classroom, sometimes you'll want to delete a class when it's the end of the semester, and you can always restore it again if you need to. You can also delete it if you never want to see that class again, or have no use for it because you've got the assignments already. Now, if you don't archive these, they will stick around, so make sure that you archive them first.

Archived classes essentially mean that they're in an area where you have the same materials the work students have, and the posts. You can view it, but you can't actually use it, and is good for if a student wants the materials.

Archiving classes is simple to do. You choose the class, see the three dots, press them, and Hey Presto! It's archived.

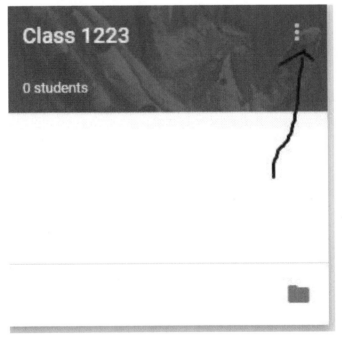

Now to view an archived class after it's been archived, you press the three-line menu again, go down to the tab that says archive classes, and then choose the class you want to see.

To delete a class though, you essentially need to do the same thing. Remember, that you need to archive the class before you can delete it, so scroll all the way down, choose archive classes, and from there, once you have the classes, you need to press the three dots option, and then choose delete this. From there, you'll have the class fully removed. Remember though, you can't undo this once you've done it, and if you do choose to delete a class, you don't have access to the comments or the posts, but if you have any files that are in the drive, you can always access those, since you have those in the class files themselves.

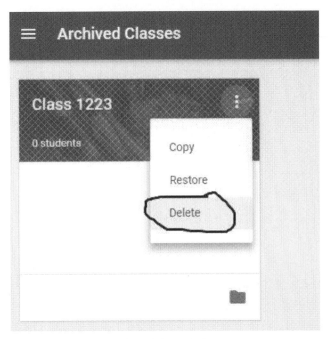

Other Tips and Tricks for Class Management

There are a few class management things that you can implement, and some tips and tricks that go into Google Classroom. The first thing that happens, is that when you get to the classes tab, and you want to drag and move the classes around, you can do so. This is a good way to change the order of things, and it's quite easy to do.

Another important thing to remember too, is that you have the classroom function. It's quite handy, and if you want to change the calendar or view it, you can essentially press the icon with the calendar that's on there, and you can even check it out to see what's coming up for every single class, because some classes may do certain things at different times of the semester.

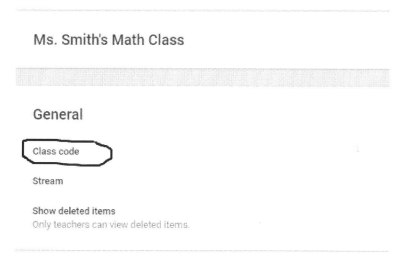

Finally, you can always adjust the settings at any point. This is done with the gear that you see on the home screen. Here, you can change the name of the class, especially if it's confusing, show the class code if you need it, and also decide on the stream and show whether or not you want items to be deleted or displayed. There are other features there too, and it's all right there waiting to be used.

Ms. Smith's Math Class

General

Class code

Stream

Show deleted items
Only teachers can view deleted items.

When it comes to Google Classroom, knowing how to create the classes is a big part of it. If you have classes that you want to add, or you want to get started with Google Classroom, this is the way to go, and it's the surefire way to success.

HOW TO INVITE STUDENTS TO GOOGLE CLASSROOM

Let's say you have the whole classroom set up, and you've put together some great assignments for the year. But what about inviting other students, teachers and even parental guardians? Well, it's super simple, will go over how you can invite both students and teachers to your classroom in order for this to work.

Having Students Join the Classroom

One of the best ways to have students join the classroom, is through a code or by an email. A code is usually the easiest one, and requires a bit less work. Plus, if you don't have the emails of each student, it's a quick and easy way to get them to set up. Now what you do is go to settings, and then choose the option to get the join code. You can then display the code to every single student, and they can log in with their Google account, press the plus button, choose to join the class and there you go, you now have students in your class. It's a much easier way, especially if you have a lot of students and you typically don't have the contact information.

If you've already got the students set up and you want to set up a personal invitation, you begin by going to the people tab (used to be students) and from there, you choose the students that you'd like to invite. If they're in a Google group already, they will be invited automatically. When you have chosen all of them, you will then send out an email to each one, and they will then have to, on their end, choose the option to accept the invite. They will then be a part of the class. If you are using the G-suite for education option, you can only add students who are in the Google domain and if the students are using public email accounts rather than school email accounts, they won't be able to access the online content. This was mostly put there to give extra security. However, it does add a bit of an extra step, so if you are in a district that doesn't have emails that are already readily available to students, usually the join code link is the better option.

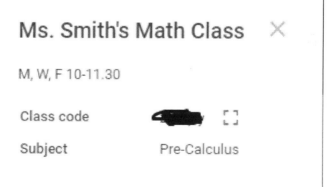

Ms. Smith's Math Class ✕

M, W, F 10-11.30

Class code

Subject   Pre-Calculus

The email is ideal to use when you have students that typically don't meet in person for classes, or maybe they do, but most of the focus is an online type of class. It's best if you make sure to encourage students to have an icon with their email address, as it does prevent the wrong person from getting the wrong contact information, and that makes it easier on everybody at the end of the day. However, you can only do the Google group if you know the email addresses of every single student who must join the class.

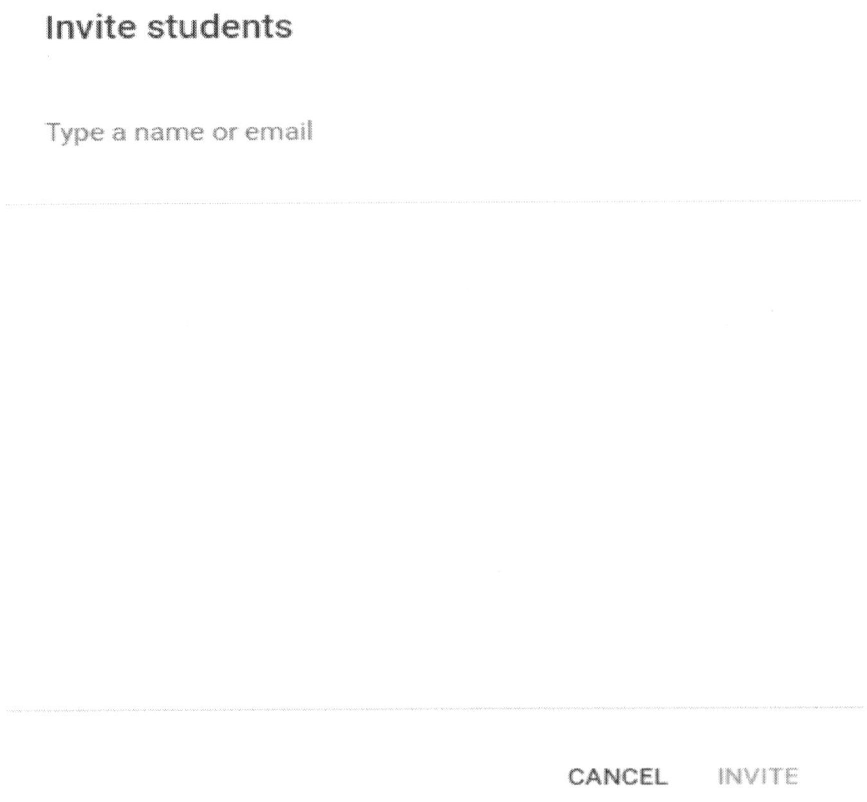

Invite students

Type a name or email

CANCEL   INVITE

Inviting Students to A Class

through email, you will ask a group of students to enter your level. However, you must first build a group of students in your Gmail account

Step 1

Click the "students" button at the top of the page.

Step 2

Select "invite"

Step 3

Pick a group of students that you would like to invite.

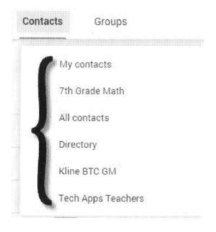

Step 4

Click "Pick All" then "Invite Students" Add Students by Code

Adding Teachers to Google Classrooms

If you have a student teacher, or maybe a co-teacher that you collaborate with, having this extra little addition is pretty good, since you can have consistency among each of the classes. With this, you can make sure that you have responsible, simple posting in each of the classes. However, because Google classroom doesn't have the automatic option to add teachers, you need to make sure that you manually do so. That's because usually each class is viewed as an individual, but if you work together, you need to have both options. However, it's very easy to add a teacher to this class.

Invite teachers

Type a name or email

Teachers you add can do everything you can, except delete the class.

First, you go to the about tab, and choose the option to invite the teacher. From here, the teacher will need to accept the invite themselves, and once they do, they will be able to access the class and help the teacher with various aspects

HOW TO USE THE QUESTION FEATURE

Google Classroom offers a forum for teachers to share their class announcements. Teachers can publish announcements on the stream or send an email to Gmail accounts of the students. Learners can retrieve older notifications by scrolling down in their stream. Apart from verbal notices or those penned on a whiteboard, Google Classroom announcements are available outside the classroom environment. The Google Classroom also lets students reply to the announcement as well. That changes what conventionally could be one-way communication into two-way communication.

Steps for generating Announcements:

1. Press the + on the monitor at the lower right corner

2. Select Create an Announcement option

3. Attach the announcement description

4. Pick the class(s) you would like to see the notification

5. Include files, folders, or connections as required

6. Tap POST to attach to the stream, or save as a draft for later posting

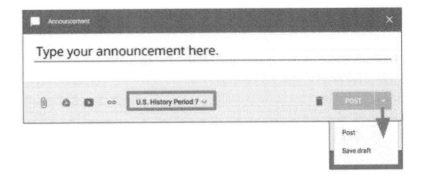

Create a Discussion Question:

1. Tap the + in the lower right corner and then select the Create Question option

2. Insert the content of your query and a summary if needed

3. Give a due date

4. Choose the class(s) you wish to ask the question to

5. Provide files, folders, or links to other websites for additional help

6. Press ASK to connect to the list or save as a draft for later posting

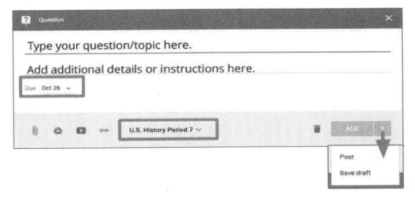

7. When you press ASK, you would see a pop-up with the "Let students ..." choices below

a. See and return each other's responses

b. Edit their responses

Pick your choices, then press on ASK.

Student's View: Announcements & Questions:

All the announcements will appear in the student's stream and are usually read-only; however, if the instructor has allowed this, students have the choice to make a class statement. The teacher and all students that are part of the class can watch class posts. The students may also access the data, connections, or clips if the announcement has any attachments.

Student's View of Questions in the Stream:

Once the students are given a topic for discussion, it should be shown in the Stream instantly. Students are going to see the below stream options.

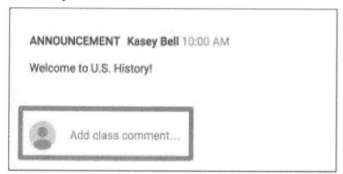

• Final state (not finished or accomplished)

• Deadline Date (Students can even see if the assignment given is late).

• Name and Summary of discussion

• Your response: This is where participants put in their answers. Students must first send their answers before they can access the answers from other classmates

• Add a Class Message: Use this room to ask difficult questions or to reply to other's quires generally. This is NOT where you type in your answers the questions provided by your instructor

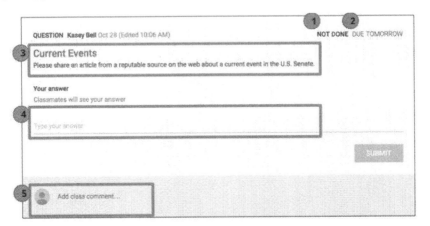

Note: The question's heading is clickable and will transfer students to a specific page for that topic. Students may also have the choice to put in their answer on this tab, but they will now have the opportunity to make a personal message, which the instructor can only access. Make sure students Comprehend to enter their answers in the answer reply field, and not as comment as well as personal reply.

Share Resources:

Google Classroom lets teachers to take a file, video, or link and push it out to their students. Using Google Classroom as a consistent location for users to acquire electronic resources maximizing the time required for classroom teaching. The classroom environment is improved when students are not driven to different places to locate required resources.

Click the "Announcement" button at the top of the Google Classroom stream to share your resource. There are 4 icons at the bottom edge of the creation box for announcements.

•   The paper clip symbol attaches saved files on to the computer

•   The Google Drive icon requires the announcement to be added to the announcement from Google Docs or any files saved in the Google Drive of teacher. If the file is stored personally in Google Drive, the sharing settings are changed to allow students in the class to access the file without the instructor taking any further action

•   The YouTube icon enables the teacher to upload the URL of a YouTube video they've already found. Conversely, a search box for locating YouTube videos is available in Google Classroom

•   The fourth icon lets the teacher upload an Internet resource URL

Documents shared in Google Classroom through the Announcements tool are shared as view-only documents with the students. Unless the teacher also decided to share these resources at other places besides Google Classroom, these resources are not visible to classmates not in the class.

Create a Lesson:

Google Classroom enables the instructor to construct a comprehensive lecture, rather than simply assigning tasks to the students. The teacher may click on "Assignment" at the top of the Classroom stream option to start creating a lesson series. The assignment's summary area enables the instructors to give students instructions for finishing the lesson and its related assignment.

Students are capable of moving more effectively through the lecture when the resources and materials are provided in a logical sequence. The lesson set may be started by making and adding an instructional file in Google Drive by using Google Drive symbol.

To supplement the instructional file, the instructor may add the subsequent part of the lesson set to YouTube videos or videos located on the Google Drive of the teacher. Engaging in video clips, screencasts, or short pieces of guidance may provide additional understanding beyond the instructional text. In addition, videos may be used to differentiate instructions for learners. Supplying numerous videos addressing different teaching methods or ability levels can help students choose an educational solution that suits them.

Websites which enable learners to perform some of the lecture skills can be provided as part of the lecture set. In addition, co-creative documents can be introduced to the lecture set to allow brainstorming or crowd-source information for the students. The very last part of the lesson set usually is the student's assignment to finish. Adding a pictorial organizer, or blueprint document given to the student for completing the task.

HOW TO INTEGRATE APPS

While Google Classroom can be used by anyone wanting to teach and learn, essentially, it is built for schools, so having an ID for the G Suite and accessing the site via the ID helps keep things organized in the online sphere for administration purposes in a school. It ensures that you do not mix your private and personal documents and information into your Google Drive or Gmail account connected to your suite.

TES Teach

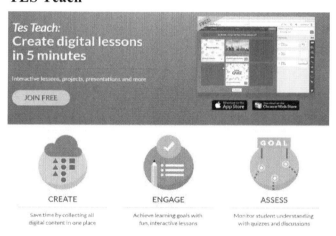

TES Teach is one of those must-have applications to integrate with your Google Classroom as it has plenty of lessons, presentations, and projects. You can create interactive content using TES Teach and use it on your Google Classroom.

Discovery Education

Discovery Education is another source of well-curated information loaded into digital textbooks, digital media, and Virtual Field Trips that feature content that is relevant and dynamic. They also have easy-to-use tools and resources that enable teachers to include it in their differentiated learning modules to improve their student's achievements.

cK-12

You can download this app either in student mode or teacher mode. If you plan on creating a differentiated assignment, then this website is your Holy Grail because it is filled with a library of online textbooks, flashcards, exercises videos, and all of it is for free!

GeoGebra

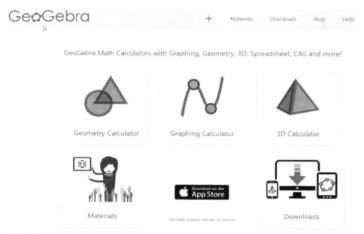

GeoGebra is an excellent app for both educators and students alike. It includes a graphing calculator, 3D calendar, and geometry calculator that can be used to produced geometry, calculus, statistics, and 3D math and functions.

Alma

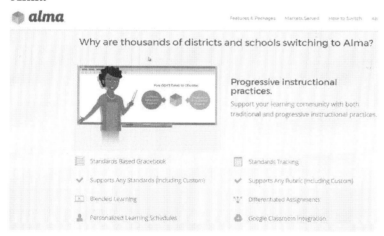

Alma is cool and sleek software designed to help schools and teachers improve their school management, learning management system, and student information system. Its interface is user-friendly, and it has systems with grading, standards tracking, and supports any kind of Rubric.

Buncee

The Tool that Fosters Creativity

Easy to use for students of all ages, Buncee encourages them to reach their full potential. Create a fun learning environment in the classroom while engaging students both at home and at school.

Visualize

Easily bring your critical thinking and creativity to life.

Encourage your student's creativity through Buncee, a presentation tool that is highly interactive and loaded with an extensive list of visualization components. Buncee allows students as well as educators to create highly visual and interactive presentation stickers, animation, and built-in templates. Buncee is currently used in over 127 countries.

Google Cultural Institute

The Google Cultural Institute features an online collection of art, exhibits, and archives sourced from around the world. Need to link an assignment with content? Look it up on Google Cultural Institute. You can find an extensive list of topics and articles categorized under experiments, historical figures and events, movements as well as artists curated from museums and archives worldwide.

Curiosity.com

With the goal to ignite the curiosity and inspire, this app curates and creates content for millions of learners all around the world. Editors look for content and present it in the best way possible. Curiosity can be accessed through the website or through their app.

Duo Lingo

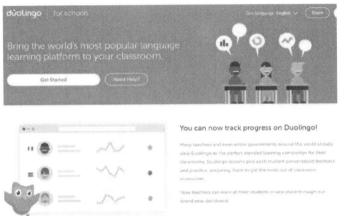

Duo lingo is, by far, the world's most popular language website. For schools, Duo Lingo is the ideal-blended learning companion for their classrooms all around the world. Duo lingo lessons give personalized feedback and practice to each student, preparing them to get the most out of classroom instruction.

Ed Puzzle

To be used by both educators as well as learners, Ed Puzzle allows you to create your own videos and include interactive lessons, voice over, audio, and many more to turn any video into a lesson. What's more, teachers can also track if a student watches the videos, the answers they give, and how many times they view a video.

Edulastic

Edulastic is a platform that allows for personalized formative assessment for K-12 students, teachers, and school districts. It gives educators a highly interactive, cloud-based learning environment and gives deeper insights into the students' understanding of a subject.

Flat

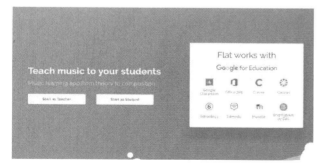

Flat is a great application to use for music teachers who want to create music notation and composition assignments. You can integrate Google Classroom with Flat Education and synchronize existing rosters on your Classroom as well as design new activities that students can access via Classroom.

Learn Zillion

This website is the world's first curriculum-as-a-service program that utilizes digital curricular materials and combines it with an enterprise platform as well as professional services to enable districts and states to effectively manage their curricula and provide their teachers with the best tools to make engaged and blended learning possible.

Listen wise

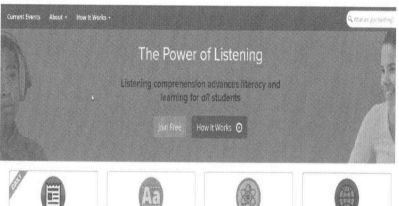

This listening skills platform harnesses the power of listening to empower learning and literacy for students. This site features podcasts and public radio content.

Lucid Press

Encourage your students to create visually stunning materials for their assignments using Lucid Press. From newsletters to brochures, digital magazines to online flyers, Lucid Press incorporates an intuitive interface of drag-and-drop that is easy for beginners and also for experienced designers.

Near pod

Create intuitive lessons with Near pod whether in ppt, jpeg, or PDF files and upload them to your Google Classroom. Near pod enables teachers to create mobile presentations and share and control the presentation in real time.

Newsela

With Newsela, you can integrate articles into your assignments with embedded assessments. Start a dialogue, customize prompts, and facilitate close reading with this app.

PBS Learning Media

The PBS Learning Media is a standards-aligned digital resource that gives educators and students access to digital resources both for student and professional development.

Pear Deck

This tool enables each student in your class to connect to your presentation on any device. When connected, they can answer your interactive questions and learn from their peers simultaneously.

HOW TO MANAGE STUDENTS

Alongside guidance and evaluation, assignments form the establishment of the instructing and learning process. They give chances to students to rehearse the aptitudes and apply the information that they have been educated in a strong domain. It likewise enables the teacher to check how well students are learning the material and that they are so near authority.

As a result of the idea of assignments, overseeing them can get feverish. That is the reason its best to utilize a platform like Google Classroom to assist you with overseeing assignments carefully. In the present tip, we will examine 48 different ways that you can utilize the Classroom to manage student assignments.

Task Status – Effectively check what number of students turned in a task just as what number of assignments have been reviewed by setting off to the Classwork tab and tapping on the title of the task.

Appoint to Numerous Classes – Post a task to different classes by utilizing the "for" drop-down menu while making a task.

Conceptualize – Use Google Docs, Sheets, Slides, or Drawings to conceptualize for class assignments.

Calendar of Due Dates – Connection a Google Calendar with due dates for assignments, tests, and other significant dates into the Classroom.

Check Schoolwork – Classroom makes checking schoolwork simple with a brisk look at the task page. In the event that increasingly nitty-gritty reviewing is required, simply get to the evaluating interface for the task.

Decision Sheets – Give students a decision by the way they exhibit what they know by making a decision board and transferring it as a task. Decision sheets permit students to pick between a few assignments and can be made legitimately in the Classroom, utilizing Google Docs, or with outsider applications.

Co-Show Classes – Welcome others to co-educate in your Classroom. Every teacher can make assignments and post declarations for students.

Make Inquiries Before a Socratic Workshop – Make a task for students to create inquiries before a Socratic class. During the community-oriented procedure, students can take out copy questions.

Detainment Task Sheet – Make a confinement task sheet utilizing Google Docs. The task sheet would then be able to be imparted to the detainment teacher and individual students secretly through the Classroom.

Separate Assignments – Allot work to singular students or gatherings of students in the Classroom.

The separate result – Separate side-effect in the Classroom by giving a test, assortment, or decision or by utilizing a continuum with assignments.

Advanced Portfolios – Students can make computerized arrangement of their work by transferring reports, pictures, curios, and so on to Classroom assignments.

Bearings Report – Use Google Docs to make guidance records for assignments in the Classroom.

Appropriate Student Work/Schoolwork – Use Classroom to disperse student assignments or schoolwork to all students, gatherings of students, or individual students.

Enhance Student Entries – Make elective accommodation alternatives for students through the task tool. For instance, one gathering of students might be required to present a Google Doc while another gathering is required to present a Slides introduction.

Do-Now Exercises – Use Classroom to post Do-Now Exercises.

Draft Assignments – Save posts as drafts until they are prepared for distributing.

Input Before Student Submits – Give criticism to students while their task is as yet a work in progress as opposed to holding up until accommodation. This will enable the student to all the more likely to comprehend task desires.

Get Informed Generally Assignments – Select warning settings to get advised each time a task is turned in late.

Worldwide Classroom – Join forces with global teachers to make a co-encouraging classroom without outskirts where students can deal with community assignments.

Realistic Coordinators – Transfer realistic coordinators for students to work together on assignments and activities.

Gathering Coordinated effort – Dole out different students to a task to make a community-oriented gathering. Give students altering rights to permit them access to a similar archive.

HyperDocs – Make and transfer a hyperdoc as a task.

Connection to Assignments – Make connects to assignments not made in the Classroom.

Connection to Class Blog – Give the connection to a class blog in the Classroom.

Connection to Next Action – Give a connection to the following movement students must finish in the wake of completing a task.

Make a Duplicate for Every Student – Picked "make a duplicate for every student" while transferring task archives to maintain a strategic distance from students sharing one duplicate of the record. At the point when a duplicate for every student is made, Classroom naturally adds every student's name to the archive and saves it to the Classroom folder in Google Drive.

Move to Top/Base – Move late assignments to the highest point of the Classwork feed so students can discover new errands all the more rapidly.

Different File Transfer – Transfer numerous files for a task in one post.

Naming Shows for Assignments – Make a novel naming framework for assignments so they can be handily found in the Classroom folder in Google Drive.

Disconnected Mode – Change settings to permit students to work in disconnected mode if web associations are frail. When a web association is set up, students can transfer assignments to the Classroom.

One Student One Sheet – In Google Sheets, appoint one tab (sheet) per student for the student to finish the task.

One Student One Slide – In Google Slides, appoint one slide to every student to introduce discoveries on a theme or to finish a task.

Compose Student Work – Google Classroom consequently makes calendars and folders in Drive to keep assignments sorted out.

Companion Coaches – Dole out friend guides to help battling students with assignments.

Secure Protection – Google Classroom just permits class individuals to get to assignments. Likewise, it takes out the need to utilize email, which might be less private than the Classroom.

Give Lodging – Furnish facilities to students with incapacities in Google Classroom by permitting additional opportunity to turn in assignments, utilizing content to discourse capacities, and outsider extensions for shaded overlays.

Reorder Assignments by Status – Rather than sorting out assignments by the student's first or last name, arrange them by status to see which students have or have not turned in work.

Reuse Posts – Reuse posts from earlier assignments or from different Classrooms.

See the Procedure – Students don't need to present their assignments for you to see their work. At the point when you picked "make a duplicate for every student" for assignments, every student's work can be found in the reviewing tool, regardless of whether it's not submitted. Teachers can offer remarks and recommendations en route.

Offer Materials – Transfer required materials, for example, the class schedule, rules, strategies, and so on to a Class Assets Module, or transfer task materials inside the task.

Offer Assets – Make an asset list or an asset module for students.

Offer Answers for a Task – Offer answers for a task with a teammate or students after the sum total of what assignments have been turned in.

Quit Rehashing Bearings – By presenting aheading archive on assignments, the need to persistently rehash bearings is reduced, if not disposed of by and large. Remember that a few students will in any case need headings to peruse orally or explained.

Student Work Assortment – Use the Classroom to gather student work from assignments.

Summer Assignments – Make summer assignments for students in the Classroom.

Formats – Make layouts for undertakings, expositions, and other student assignments.

Track Assignments Turned In – Monitor which students turned in assignments by heading off to the reviewing tool.

HOW TO USE THE GOOGLE SLIDES

Introducing Google Slides in Your Classroom

If you have been using Microsoft PowerPoint, you will have a clearer idea of what Google Slides is. PowerPoint is often used for creating presentation slides.

Google Slides is closely related to PowerPoint, but unlike PowerPoint, it is hosted online and allows many people to collaborate and work on the same presentation at the same time. Here are some quick facts about Google Slides:

Google Slides is free

• There is a blank document you can start your presentation in, or you can make use of pre-designed templates.

• You can access it via the web on all internet-enabled devices like PC, Android, iOS, etc. or as a desktop application on Google Chrome OS.

• You can easily import PowerPoint files into Google Slides and then edit them. Amazingly, slides can be exported as PowerPoint files, PDF, JPEG, or PNG files.

• You can add images, audio, and video to presentations.

• The sharing options for Google Slides are numerous. You can make it private, or you can select a few people to share it with, or you can even make it available for a wider public. You can also choose if people can only view or view and edit the presentation.

- When collaborating with others on Google Slides, you can chat with them, leave comments, and work together on the slide at the same time.

- Saving your work as your presentation is automatic.

- You can first present your slide within the Slides (View > Present). You can also connect your system to a screen or make use of AirPlay or Chromecast in showing the presentation to a live audience.

- The presentation can also be done live on Hangout.

- You can quickly add captions to your work while presenting on Google Slides.

- Google Slides comes with numerous add-ons. These third-party tools enable you to get more functions on your Google Slides. Most of them are free, while some are premium versions.

- You can embed Google Slides in blogs and websites

How to Prepare a Google Slide Presentation?

If you try the method provided above for starting a Google Slide presentation, you will have the option to build a blank presentation or use a pre-designed template. Irrespective of the options, everyone can conveniently and easily create a presentation.

Below are some essentials that will help you create an excellent Google Slides presentation.

- Include Text through Text Boxes (you can drag and drop wherever you like)

- Insert important elements using the Insert function on the main toolbar. You can insert elements like images, videos, audio, shapes, charts, tables, word art, diagrams, or animations.

- With the (+) button, add new Slides.

- Duplicating slides can be done by right-clicking on the left navigation panel. This is easier than building slides from scratch. The duplicate function is also present under the Slide menu.

How to Use Google Slides in the Classroom

When you create a slide deck, using Google Slides becomes easier. This is the combination of several slides for the creation of a single presentation. Many use a slide deck for supporting oral presentations.

Here are some situations where teachers or students might need to make use of the basic side deck:

- Slides can be created when you wish to support the lessons presented to your students.

- If students are planning an oral presentation, they can prepare slides as part of their homework.

- Both students and teachers can also create slide decks when they need to showcase learning, or when sharing school programs like in a school assembly, information evening, etc. are needed.

- Collaboration on the slide deck can be required for conferences and staff meeting presentations.

217

These are some of the things you can do with Google Slides, and they are just some of the basics.

HOW TO SET UP AUTO-GRADE FOR GOOGLE FORMS

The first thing you'll need to create a google form is a Gmail account. You must be signed in to your Gmail account before you can create a google form. Also note that any google form you create is linked to the Gmail account that is signed in as at the time you created the google form.

All your google forms are saved on your Google drive. There is a Google drive for every Gmail account created, with 15Gb of free storage space which can be expanded upon request. That's why you need to know the Gmail address you are signed in to before creating your Google forms.

1. **Creating a Google Form**

To create a new Google form, you'll need;

a) A Gmail addresses

b) A browser

c) An internet connection

Note: Most of the explanations here are accompanied with laptop/desktop images, and may differ when creating google forms with mobile phones.

Step 1

Open your browser, and type the URL (https://google.com/forms)

Step 2

Click on "Blank quiz". But If you aren't creating a quiz, just a normal form that won't require grading, you should click on just "Blank".

Step 3

If you clicked on "Blank", you should see an empty form like the one below. Click on the "untitled form" at the top left corner of the form, and change to a more suitable title. However, this title is only the name given to the form for storage purpose.

The "untitled form" (above form description) on the white field will automatically change to the title you gave above. You may however still change this title, as it is the name your students will see when filling your form.

Step 4

Form description: You can use this field to give instructions to your students such as "Answer all questions in this quiz" or "Ensure you complete this test alone and submit before Monday".

2.   Styling Your Google Form

Styling your Google form is probably one of the most neglected part of creating a google form, but for teachers, this is a point of attraction. Follow the steps below to style your google form.

Step 1
Click on the theme/palette symbol at the top right corner of the form to change the theme of the form. With this palette, you can also change the background color and font style of your form.

Step 2

Click on "choose image to change the header of your form. A box will open with preinstalled images to choose from for your header (see image below). Or you can click on "upload photos" to select a picture from your computer.

Click here to change theme color if you are not using an image for the header

Click here to change the font style of your form.

Getting Started with Asking Questions

The Form template has one question field already on it when it opens. To add more questions, click on the + sign in the right tool box.

These are the different question types available.

The default field is set up for a Multiple-Choice question. To change the question type, click on the down-arrow (beside multiple choice) to reveal the drop-down menu. YOU SHOULD ALWAYS CREATE A SHORT ANSWER FIELD FIRST FOR THE STUDENT'S NAME. Adding the NAME field first BEFORE your questions are added will place the student's name in the FIRST column of the spreadsheet that shows student's answers/responses

The question type selections are –

Short Answer - Works well for short, written text responses. Best for responses that won't require long text. Ex. – First Name; last name; School; Class; Age; Short sentences; short phrases; spelling tests.

Paragraph - This question type works well for longer, written text responses/answers. Ex. – Essay responses; responses to writing prompts; summaries.

Multiple Choice - Respondents pick one option from choices. Multiple choice question type can also be used to create true/false responses by labeling one choice true and one choice false. Google form automatically creates options for you in multiple choice based on its understanding of your question. You may choose to use it or create yours. You create more options by clicking the "Add option" NOT "Add other".

Checkboxes - - This question type lets respondents pick as many options as they'd like. In other words, when there may be more than one answer. An example of the use of this question type could be "choose all that apply".

Dropdown - This question type works well when there is a long list of choice options, e.g. State of Origin, Nationality, etc. This question type also works well for sequencing.

File Upload: This type allows the student upload certain documents such as pictures or videos. You can select the different document formats that the student can upload and the maximum file size. This feature is valuable when you want your students to submit their workings or when requesting for CVs.

Linear Scale - This question type lets the respondent rank something along a designated scale of numbers. Scales are good to use for rubrics, peer and general evaluations. The highest number on the scale rating question type is 10, while the least is 0. Most people use 1-5 as their range. 1 can represent Poor while 5 can represent Excellent.

Multiple-Choice Grid - a grid can work as a scale for more than one question and response. If used as a scale, it takes up less space on a form than placing a scale for each question. You can also create a grid for multiple choice responses.

Checkbox Choice Grid: This works the same as multiple choice grid, except that more than one option can be chosen. You can however limit the response to "one choice per column".

Date – This field is to insert a date into your Form. By default, a calendar pops up when this field is to be filled. This option is suitable for questions like Date of Birth.

Time – This field enables the respondent to insert the time into your Form.

225

QUESTION TOOLBOX

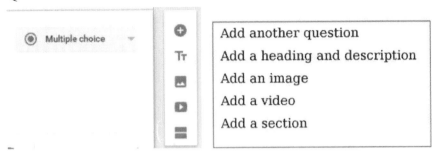

You're probably already familiar with what the + sign does. You use it to add new questions to your forms. The others are explained briefly below.

Heading & Description (TT)

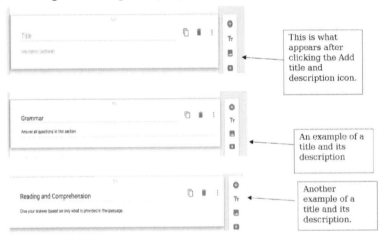

This feature is used to break your quiz into thematic chunks. Each "chunk" can then be labeled with a heading, and a description can be added for instructions. For example, if I were giving a Form quiz on English Language, I may label one part of the quiz with the heading, Grammar, and another part with

Reading and Comprehension.

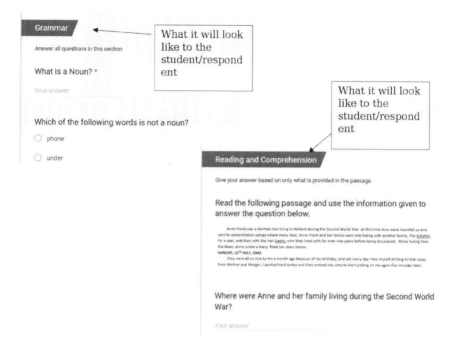

Adding an Image

You can insert images into your Form to use as writing prompts. For example, if I were a Biology teacher (which I certainly am not), and I wanted to give a quiz based on a topic I recently taught such as Flowering plant. I could get a picture of the plant, with certain parts already labelled.

Steps: Click on add image; a dialogue box opens; select "chose an image to upload"; After selecting the image, add title to the image such as Parts of a Flowering Plant (this title is different from the "title and description learnt" above). The image can be resized (smaller or bigger). It can also be aligned to the left, right, or center, by clicking on the 3 dots at the top-left side of the image.

You could then "add a question" accompanying the image such as "which of the following is the part labelled B? (of cos, you already know this should be a multiple-choice question).

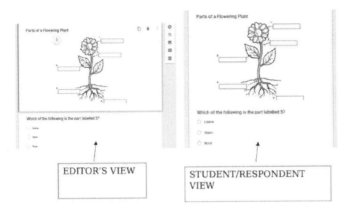

If you have the direct website link to the image, you can also paste it in the URL field, and it will be automatically uploaded.

Adding a Video

You can add a YouTube video for instructional purposes. Once you've selected the add video option, you can select a video from your computer just like it was explained for adding pictures. Alternatively, you can search YouTube for the particular video you want within the dialog box, or paste in a direct URL to the YouTube video. A question can then follow, as we learnt in "adding image".

Adding a Section

Adding sections lets you break down your quiz into separate pages, with a NEXT button to move to the next Form page. Please note that this is different from the "header and description"

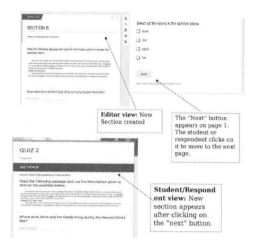

Editor view: New Section created

The "Next" button appears on page 1. The student or respondent clicks on it to move to the next page.

Student/Respondent view: New section appears after clicking on the "next" button.

3.   Question Settings/Options

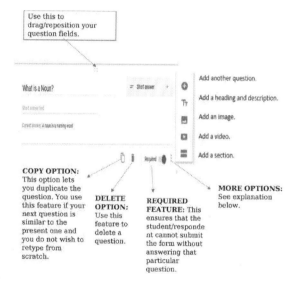

Use this to drag/reposition your question fields.

Add another question.

Add a heading and description.

Add an image.

Add a video.

Add a section.

COPY OPTION: This option lets you duplicate the question. You use this feature if your next question is similar to the present one and you do not wish to retype from scratch.

DELETE OPTION: Use this feature to delete a question.

REQUIRED FEATURE: This ensures that the student/respondent cannot submit the form without answering that particular question.

MORE OPTIONS: See explanation below.

Note: The illustration above explains the different tools you will see constantly around your question, and how to use them.

See more below.

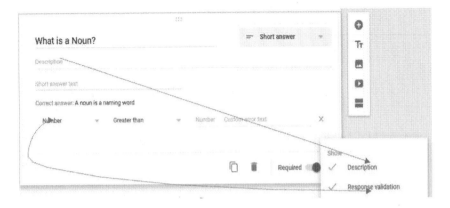

More Options: When you click on the three dots below your question, certain options will pop out (which we can call MORE OPTIONS), depending on the question type. Some of these options appear based on the question type.

For example, under Short Answer and other question types, we have,

1) Description: This can be used when you feel that a brief explanation needs to be given to enable the student or the respondent understand the question asked better. Checking this feature makes the description field appear under the question.

2) Response Validation: This feature ensures that the student/respondent only inputs certain features before he/she can submit the form. The response validation available for now includes;

a)   Number: If you want the student to input a value within a certain range. For example, you can ask your students "how many bones do we have in the human body"? The answer is 206. You therefore select a response validation of "number", then choose from the number range options (greater than, less than, etc.), then enter the value depending on range option selected. Custom error text is simply the message the student receives if his/her answer doesn't fall within your selected range.

b)   Text: This feature ensures that the student inputs or doesn't input certain characters. Have you ever tried to create a password and you were prompted to use a password with uppercase, lowercase, etc. Yeah! That's it! This has four kinds of validation. i) Contains: When you want the student to input certain text. ii) Doesn't Contain: When you want to ensure that the student doesn't put in certain text. Both "contain" and "doesn't contain" must be specified in the "text" field following it. iii) Email: This ensures that a valid email address (with @ and .com or .xxx) is put in when asking for email addressing. iv) URL: This ensures that a valid website address is put into the answer field.

c)   Length: This feature ensures that the student doesn't put in more than the specified number of characters. E.g. when asking for phone numbers, you can set this length to Minimum of 9 (for telephones) or Maximum of 14 for mobile phones with +234.

d)   Regular expression: This is almost the same as text but differs because it contains "matches" and "not matches" feature. So, the answer the student gives won't just contain certain words but may or may not match certain words.

Note: Whichever question the above features appear, they mean the same thing.

3) Shuffle Option Order: This feature ensures that every respondent doesn't see each question option in the same order. This is particularly helpful to teachers, as it helps you checkmate cheating

amongst your students. This feature will show as "shuffle row order" for multiple or checkbox choice grid.

4) Go to section based on answer: This feature is used when you want the next question only to appear based on the answer of the previous question. So, you can select where each option will take you to if selected, either to a submit button or to a new section or to page 2 of the form

HOW TO CREATE A CLASSROOM

The structure of the distance course on the platform, Google Classroom.

We will now get acquainted with the basic elements of Google Classroom on the example of the "My course in Google Class" remote training.

When creating and organizing a course, you will have three main tabs available: Ribbon, Tasks and Users. At first, you will see only two tabs:

1.   Tape

2.   Users.

You will need to add the "Tasks" tab to the course.

For a start, let us understand what a ribbon is. This is the place where current information on the course is collected and displayed: training materials, announcements, tasks and user comments are visible.

The TASKS tab allows you to add training materials to the course and distribute tasks according to topics and in the required sequence.

In the USERS section, there will be a list of trainees who have joined the course. This can be done by code or by adding manually. The course code can be found by clicking on the gear image.

Distance course in Google Classroom

Tape: information about what is happening in the course

233

The tape displays what is happening in the course in the sequence in which the teacher adds information to the course:

1.   Teacher announcements

2.   Information about training materials for students

3.   Information about the tasks for students

4.   Announcements from the students themselves. This requires additional settings.

Ribbon in Google Classroom

When creating Ads, the teacher can add different material in addition to the text, attach a file (it needs to be downloaded from a computer), add a file from Google Drive, publish a link to a video from YouTube or give a link to an external site.

Students have the opportunity to view the Announcements and comment on this. If you need to add an advertisement, then you should use "Add a new entry".

Adding to the Google Classroom

It should be noted that all the downloaded material in the Course Tape in the new entry section is placed in the course folder on Google Drive. You can see the folder in the "Tasks" tab.

If you do not want your students to comment on your recording, you can disable/enable this in the Course Settings section. You will find this in the upper right corner of the course page where the gear is. There you can enable students to leave entries in the course feed or prevent them from doing so by clicking on disable.

To create the "Tasks" tab on your training course, click on the "?" in the lower left.

This is a new tab in Google Classroom. In the "Tasks" tab you can:

1.   Create tasks and questions, and group them by topic

2.   Add educational materials of various types and combine them by topic

3.   Organize the topics and materials in them; if the material does not have a topic, it is located at the top of the page.

Tasks for students can be of various types. The teacher can attach as a Task any document located on a PC or on Google Drive, and give a link to a video. You can also offer to perform practical work or test work in the form of a test, or add a question that both teachers and other students will be able to comment on. For this, you need certain settings.

Currently, it is possible to create Tasks using Google Forms. Google Forms is very versatile and with its help, it is easy to create tests with a choice of one or several answers, open tasks and create tasks using pictures and videos, etc.

Tasks can have a set deadline. After students complete the assignments, information about this is automatically sent to the teacher. To view past assignments, the teacher goes to the TAPE section, then clicks All Tasks.

The teacher will receive information about the submitted / non-submitted work.

The teacher can check students' assignments, set grades and comment on students' answers.

As a rule, after creating a course the author creates a landing page in which he briefly presents a description of the course — the program, the start and end date of the course, the rules of work and requirements for students and a link to the registration form.

The author of the course sends the Course code to all those registered on the landing page, then students themselves are added to the course or you can manually invite students to the course. You can do this in the "Users" tab where you can see the Course Code and invite students by name or email address.

We remind you that students must have a Google account for classes in a training course organized on the Google Classroom platform!

HOW TO CREATE AND COLLECT ASSIGNMENTS FOR STUDENTS

Obviously, a big part of teaching is assignments and homework. Managing all of this is a big part of teaching, will go over everything you need to know about managing it, including streams, announcements, homework, assignments, and how you can manage it all easily.

The Stream

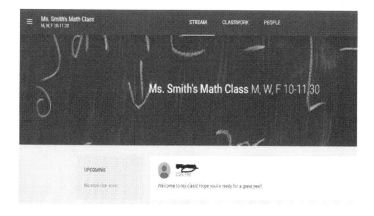

First thing we will discuss is the stream. This is essentially how communication is managed at this point. If you're familiar with social media, this is essentially like Facebook, and it's how members of each class communicate, and both teachers and students use it. Of course, if you have a class that has questions, you can essentially just respond to the question as it's asked.

To begin, once you have a class made you press the plus button, and from there choose the option to create a post. If you don't see it highlighted, that means that someone turned off posts. You can write the comment, and then post it. From there you can add attachments through pressing the paperclip that you see and then you can add that as an attachment to the stream.

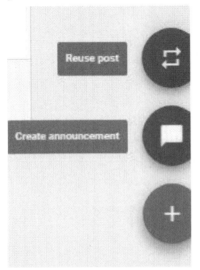

There are other options too. You can create an announcement, an assignment, a question, or even reuse posts whenever possible. Just choose the option, and then you can then post it. Attaching a topic to this is another great option too.

Scheduling and Reusing Posts

Scheduling and reusing posts is something teachers do, especially if they have an assignment they liked. To schedule a post, you can create it so that it appears at a specific time and date. To do this, you press the option to create a post or assignment, and then on the side, you'll see a tab that has a plus sign on it. Press that, and you'll then be given the option to schedule it. From there, you can put in when it should appear on the stream, and it will happen. You can then finish up, and there you go. This is great for teachers who don't want to have to spend copious amounts of time scheduling.

Emailing students

Some teachers like to email students instead of just commenting on streams and such. If that's the case, you can go to the students tab. Usually, they show the names, and you can choose the student/s to email, and then you'll see three dots, which from there gives you the action to email students. Students can email the teacher by going to the three dots next to the name of the teacher, and from there, Gmail will open automatically and the teacher's email address will be in there. They can also go to the students' tab, choose the student and then go to the three dots and choose to email the student. This is not an ideal way to communicate, but it's one way to do so.

Announcements

Announcements are great ways to communicate general information to the class, whether it be saying hello, making sure to remind them of something, or even giving them some information to help them better understand a project or subject in class. To do this, you need to press the plus sign on the right corner, and when you're given options, choose the option to create an announcement. From there you can attach files using the paperclip option once again, or even use various links to sources that you've found. It's quite easy, and it certainly does the job.

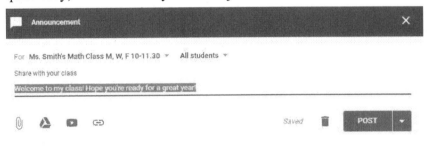

Lots of teachers like the announcement system, and students can comment on there to any announcement that they see unless you've turned it off. Students can also use it to communicate with you. If you're just now getting used to using it, you should use it as an introductory device. You can put a welcome announcement, have the students comment, or just write how you're excited to be their teacher this year. You can also tell students that commenting is super helpful for this, and that they should be able to use it easily, and learn how to master this system.

Making Assignments in Google Classroom

Making assignments and homework is a massive part of any teacher's job. Did you know that they are pretty simple to make though? The first thing that you'll want to do when you title these, is always to make sure that you have a number on them, such as 001 if you're going to have over 100 assignments for the class. This is super important, since this makes it easier for students to find the assignment in Google Classroom, and it's OK since it'll give you a chance to create an order in case you accidentally assign something out of order.

Now to begin, you need to go to the class that is to get the assignment, and from there, go to the plus sign that you see, and you'll be given the option to create an assignment.

You'll see immediately that you've been given a header. Do think carefully about this, since as soon as you assign it, you'll see a folder created for it, and the title of it matches the header, so definitely be mindful of mistakes.

Now from here, you essentially give a description of the assignment, and make sure that this is long enough for the student to go back to later, if they missed it.

You can also choose the due date for it. You essentially choose the date it's due, and it also gives you the time option, if you want it by specific time on a certain date.

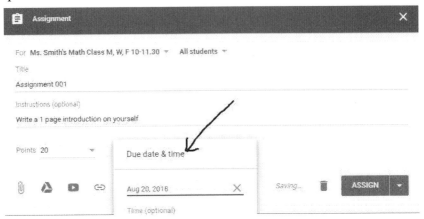

Now another big part of this is points. Lots of classes do the point system, and it's a massive part of many curriculums, and this can be changed. You can assign a point value to it by adding in manually how many points you want to add, or if you want it to be ungraded, you can use the drop-down menu to change it.

Finally, you've got the chance to add attachments. You can create templates in Google drive then add them here, and the student can then fill them out. You can give links to students too, if you want them to use a link to fill out the assignment they have.

If you want to assign this to multiple classes, you choose the class near the top, and then all of the classes to assign the work to.

Assignments in Google Drive

When using Google Classroom, sometimes teachers create assignments from the drive. For example, maybe there's a worksheet that can be used that they scan and put on the drive itself. This is actually how the resources are kept for teachers. Now, when you have an assignment that you want to put on there, you essentially need to go to Google Drive, and make sure that you choose the right option. That's because you get three different choices, and they are as follows:

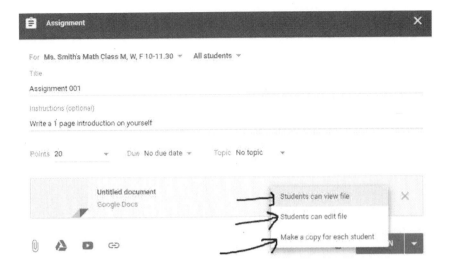

Within these options, you get the following, and these appear every time you put a Google document on there:

• Students can view the file: basically means they can look at it, but aren't allowed to modify, as in the case of study guides and handouts

• Students can edit the file: this is where they can edit the document and then work on it, which works for collaborative projects that students do together, such as various projects that they do, including group projects. Slides for an assignment are suitable for this too, or where they put together brainstorming ideas

• Make a copy: this is a way where you can choose to make a copy of the file for every single student, and they get individual editing rights for it. The master is intact, and students can't access it, but they get to fill out the other one, and this is good for any assignments that involve filling out questions, or worksheets and such.

If you're wondering whether or not you should assign it to a few, or to many, this is a good option.

Student Assignment Views

For students, it's a bit different, since they will see a different view compared to teachers. Essentially, they see the description for the assignment, and in it, a button that says open, which is where the student will put the assignment. Make sure you inform the students that they need to choose whether they are marking it as done or turning it in, depending on if they have to turn in anything or not.

How Students Interact with the Assignment

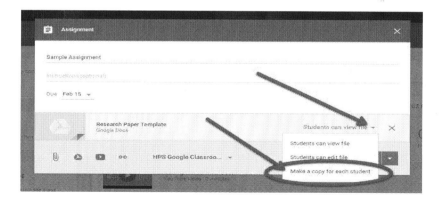

Now for students, when they choose to turn in an assignment, there are two things to realize. If you see a form with them, choose the form and answer the questions that you have, and then submit, mark it as done, and then make sure to confirm it. You'll then see that the assignment is marked as done. If you see more, you should go to open assignment, and then fill out the rest.

A document is similar in a sense. You basically do the job, turn it in, and then you'll see that when it's turned in, it'll be labeled with the name.

For attaching, you go to add on the assignment, click on the arrow, and then choose to attach a file via either drive, or a file itself. You can then attach, and turn it in.

For assignments that don't involve actually turning in anything, or maybe you want to comment on something, you touch the assignment, add the comment if needed, and then choose to mark it as done. If you have an assignment you want to change, choose it, and then press unsubmit, and there you go.

For teachers, you need to go to the pop-up menu, and it shows the assignments, and which ones will be overdue, and you can even see the grades that are there. It's an excellent way to see it, and students can also check this if they want to submit assignments.

Organizing Class Topics

With a class, you usually have different units. It can be a bit overwhelming if you don't have a decent system for it. You can however, use Topics to make it easier.

To do this, you need to go to class-work, and then under the section, press the create button, and then you can choose a topic. From there, whenever you add anything new, you can put a topic on it. You can do this with assignments as well, that are already neatly put together as needed.

The Classroom Folder

If you're a teacher who isn't sure whether or not you've given a class a particular assignment, you can check the class folder. It's located right on the home page of where the classes are listed. You can check the class folder in the Google drive.

If you want to efficiently ensure that you have a sound organization system for the students as well, you can simply make folders for all of the students at this point, and then throw the work into there each time it's put in. That way, you've got a great system, and one that works correctly for you, no matter what the odds may be.

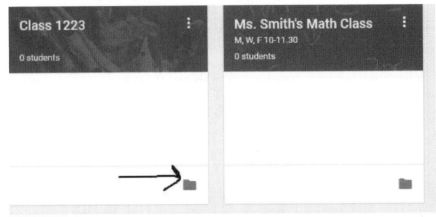

HOW TO USE QUESTIONS AND RUBRICS

Teachers can now create rubrics and use them again. As students complete their assignments, they review the logic of a task to help them stay on track. When teachers grade, level options can automatically specify a cumulative grade, which can also be changed manually. Students can quickly check their comments when they return to work.

More about rubric:

Flexible: up to 50 parameters and ten performance levels

Share: import and export options when creating jobs

Reusable: reuse a rubric in another task

Creating Rubrics

In Classroom, you can construct, reuse, move, show, and level rubrics for singular tasks.

Input can be given utilizing scored or un-scored rubrics. At the point when a rubric is scored, the students see their scores when you return their tasks.

Use fare to impart the rubrics to instructors outside of your group.

Use fare to impart the rubrics to educators outside of your group.

Make a rubric

You can develop to 50 standards for each rubric, and per basis up to 10 execution levels.

Note: The assignment must have a title before you can make a rubric.

1. Go to classroom.google.com onto a PC.

2. Snap on Classwork tab.

3. Under the rubric, make a task with a title, click on Add Rubric Build rubric.

4. Snap the change to the off situation to kill the scoring for the rubric.

5. (Discretionary) If you use scoring, pick Descending or Ascending close to sort the request for focuses.

Note: You can include the exhibition levels in any request with scoring. The rates settle consequently by point esteem.

6. Enter a class, for example, Grammar, Coordination, or Quotes, under the title Criteria.

7. (Discretionary) Include a meaning of the measures under the depiction of the model.

8. Under Ratings, enter the measure of focuses granted for the presentation level.

Note: The combined score in the rubric refreshes consequently when you include focuses.

9. Information a triumph level title under Level Title, for example, Outstanding, Absolute Mastery, or Level A.

10. Enter the necessities for the classification under Definition.

11. Click Add Grade and repeat steps 8-9 to add another level of performance to the criteria.

12. To add another criterion:

Click Add Criterion and repeat steps 6–11 to add a new criterion.

To copy a criterion, in the criteria box, click More same criteria and repeat steps 6-11.

13. To rearrange parameters at the bottom of a criteria, click More Scroll Up or Move Criterion.

14. To save your rubric, click Save in the right corner.

How to Create a Quiz

To create a test, you'll first need to produce a standard form. Navigate to the Google Forms homepage, then tap the Blank symbol.

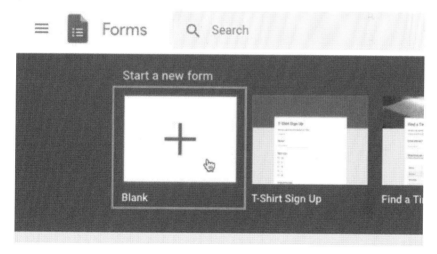

At first, you will need to include some amendments in form's settings then you can begin to write questions and answers for your quiz. Click the icon for **Settings** in the top-right corner.

Then find the **Quizzes** tab to click it as well as toggle the button for **Make this a quiz**. After doing that a lot of **quiz options** will be available for you to choose how your students will deal with your set quiz.

Then select the type of quiz setting you desire.

Source: Goodwill Community Foundation Global (2020)

Once you have actually selected your preferred setups, click Save. You can after that call your test and also begin composing your inquiries.

HOW TO USE GOOGLE CLASSROOM IF YOU'RE A STUDENT

Google Classroom was built for both the educator and learner in mind. It isn't only the teachers who can do so many things with Google Classroom, but students can also harness the full capabilities of this application. Student's reaction to Google Classroom is whenever the teacher, who is the central Manager of the Classroom, uploads content in the Classroom.

Here are some of the various things that students can do with Google Classroom.

Change Ownership

When you turn in an assignment, the teacher becomes the owner of your document. You are no longer the owner, and therefore you are unable to edit the text. Turned in the wrong assignment? Simply click on the 'Unsubmit' button. You would need to refresh Google Classroom once you un-submit so that you can resend a new document.

Assignment listings

Students can find a list of all the assignments created by teachers by clicking on the menu icon located at the top left-hand corner of Google Classroom. Practically all assignments that have not been archived can be viewed in this list.

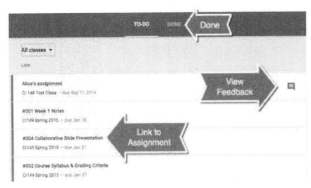

Utilize the Mobile App for more comfortable access

We know students are always on their mobile phone. One of the best ways to get notified if you have a new assignment is through the Google Classroom's mobile app. The mobile app can be downloaded and installed from the Playstore or iTunes. The app allows students to view their assignments and submit their work directly from the app. This mainly works when students are requested to submit real life samples, or a video or a combination of photos. All they need to do is take pictures of their samples or their solutions and then upload it to the Google Classroom.

No worries if you haven't clicked on Save

Encourage your students to use Google Docs to do their assignments. If you have given work that requires them to write reports, write a story or anything that requires their use of a Word document, use Google Docs because it saves edits automatically. This eliminates your student's excuses of not being able to complete their homework because they did not save it. Also, it just makes things more comfortable when you are so engrossed with completing your work, you forget to save; Google Docs does it for you.

254

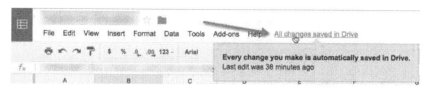

Sharing isn't the same thing as turning in

When a student clicks open an assignment to hand in their assignment, they need to click on TURN IN. Sharing an assignment to the Google Classroom is not the same thing as turning in your completed work. Make sure you click on TURN IN to submit your assignment in due time.

You will not lose assignments

Unless you delete it. Any documents you upload to your Google Classroom is only seen between you and the teacher. Any assignments you upload to your Google Drive will be seen on the teachers Google Drive as well. Your Google Drive is the storage system for Google Classroom and it works the same way for both the teacher as well as the students.

Due Dates

You'd have a more challenging time explaining to your teacher why you have not submitted your assignment especially since the due dates are continuously shown on an assignment. Assignments that are not due yet are indicated on the class tile on the home page as well as the left of the page late assignments have a particular folder, where the teacher can accurately see the assignments listing from the menu icon on the upper left of the page.

UPCOMING ASSIGNMENTS

DUE MAR 6

#016 Collaborative
Presentation

Returning an Assignment

Students working on a Google Document can return at any time to the file that they are working on. Get back to the assignment stream and click on Open and it will take you to a link to the documents that you have on Google Drive. Click on the document and get back right into it. You can also access this file directly from your personal Google Drive. It is the same way you click on any document on your desktop to work on it again. Plus, side is Google Docs auto saves.

Communicating with teachers

It's either you communicate publicly on Google Classrooms for the entire class to see, or you communicate privately. Communicating privately helps a lot especially for students who are shy and prefer to speak to the teacher directly without the involvement of other classmates. It also helps the teacher speak privately to address a student's issue on an assignment without making them feel inadequate or that they have not done well.

Commenting on Assignments

Comments on an assignment are viewable by your classmates on Google Classroom when it is made on any assignments uploaded to the app. Students just need to click on 'Add Comments' under an assignment. If students would like to communicate in private, with you, they can leave it on the assignment submission page. Within a specific document, you can use the File Menu and click on 'Email collaborators' to message or link a document to the teacher.

Add Additional files to an assignment

Students and teachers can both add additional files to an assignment. For students, they can add in files that did not come together with a template the teacher gave. You can click on ADD additional files on the assignment submission page again. Links from websites can also be added. Additional files help in the attempt to provide a wholesome blended learning approach in schools because you can add files of different formats and types

HOW TO USE GOOGLE DRIVE AND GOOGLE DOCS

The Basics of Google Drive:

The Basic features of Google Drive are the ones which almost every user will need at some point in time. So, knowing them is like a license to start up your use of Google Drive.

- **Set Up**

It is related to getting the introduction for setting up and efficient use of Google Drive.

- **Organize**

These organizing tips will help the user to consolidate the Google Drive in such a way that all the documents are easy to reach and navigate. For example, you can learn the way of adding a single file to different folders.

- **Share**

This will entail the basic working for sharing of some item on the Google Drive of one user over the Google drive of other users. You can also learn to restrict the downloading features of the shared files.

- **Delete**

This will entail the process applied for deleting a file placed on the Google Drive. You can also learn to restore the deleted file.

- **The Advanced Features of Google Drive:**

Some of the sophisticated and advanced actions include:

- **Advanced Search**

The advanced search operators of Google Drive are highly useful when the user is navigating some broader and populated Drive library.

- **View Revision History**

This feature enables the user view and effectively manages the changes which have been made to the files located on Google Drive.

- **Edit Files in Google Drive (Microsoft Files)**

The user can easily edit Microsoft files in such a way that they are eventually converted into the native Google Drive files

- **Attaching Files to an Email**

There is also an option of quickly adding the files stored in Google Drive in the email.

- **Adding a Drive Image as the Email Signature:**

Google Drive's additional capability allows you to add an image in the email signature. You can use any of the images which have been stored in the Drive. You can also learn to create the enhanced features like the signatures for company email.

- **Using Drive for Image Host**

Google Drive also entails the additional feature of hosting some image kept on Google Drive. Eventually, the image can be either be linked or directly used on the website.

- **Adding Subtitles for Videos in Google Drive**

If you have stored some videos in the Google Drive, you can also use the enhanced features of Google drive to place Subtitles on the video.

- **Managing Changes to Non-Native Files**

This enhanced feature allows the user to keep a track of all those amendments and changes which have been made to the non-native files. This also ensures that the users with whom the file is shared can only see the changed or updated file.

- **Allowing Backup for Google+ Photos**

Google Drive also keeps a backup for all the photos which the user posts on Google+.

- **Some unique features for Admins:**

As Google Drive enables plenty of domain data to get stored by all the users so it also enables the Google Apps Admins to keep a check on the security of the domain Drive.

- **Drive Security for Apps Admins**

Google Drive provides all the essential processes and related tools for Admins so that they can eventually make up a secured domain.

- **Confirmation of Drive Compliance**

The feature named Better Cloud enables the Admins to scan the domain's Drive to explore the SSNs, credit card numbers and some other form of secure information and modify and monitor the settings related to the sharing of the documents.

- **Getting Started**

In this step, you will get the most basic information for starting on with Google Drive so that the endless possibilities of this Drive can be explored in the best possible way.

Getting Access to Google Drive:

1. There can be many different methods to access the Google Drive, out of which the easiest is to use a Chrome browser. After clicking Chrome, click on a browser or on the new tab. Here you will find the page shown below. Just select the logo for Google Drive which will direct you to the website for Google Drive.

2. In case one does not have the Chrome browser then adding the appropriate URL in the search bar will also direct the user to get access to the Google Drive, as shown below:

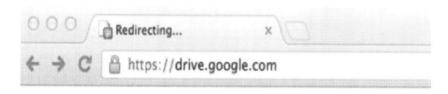

3. There can be another method for accessing Google Drive which is by searching over the Google for Google Drive.

Interface of Google Drive:

The Google Drive entails the following interface: The "My Drive" is actually in synchronization with the desktop of the user.

All of the folders appearing under My Drive will be similar to the ones which are residing within the desktop. You can use the Drag Drop function to put any of the files from the internet to "My Drive".

Desktop Application for Google Drive

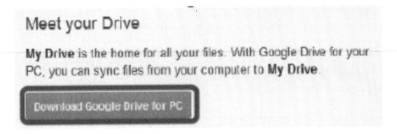

When the initial login for the Google Drive will be made, it will prompt the user to download the application for the desktop. You will need to click on the Download option.

Next, click "Accept and Install"

Click **Accept and Install**.

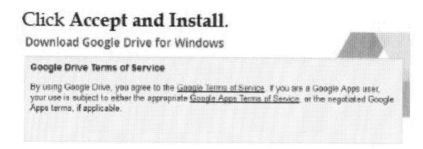

Next, click on the "Save File" icon for opening the download and proceed to "Run". It will automatically administer you to the necessary steps for downloading.

After downloading the Drive, the next step is to get signed in with a Google account. In order to start the synchronization of Google Documents with Google drive click to "Start Sync".

After this step, the Google Drive will be one of the options for saving the files. You will get a shortcut for Drive over the desktop. You can also apply a Drag- Drop function to directly add files to the drive for internet or some other source.

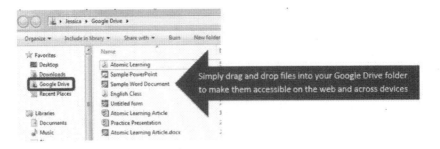

Google Drive over the Web

• There is an arrow on the left side of "My Drive", which is used to expand the Drive and show all the folders which have been synchronized with the Google Drive. Select any of the folders and its content will be displayed at the right of the screen.

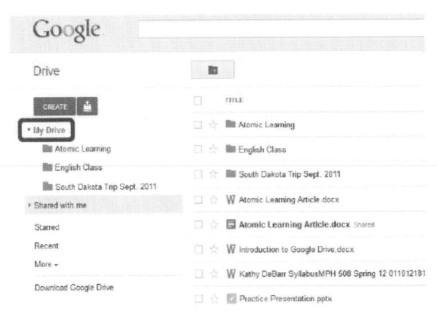

• In case you add some folder or file over the desktop, it will automatically become part of the Drive.

- Adding to folders in the "My drive" is also possible. First of all, click "Create "and from the drop down options and select the "Folders" options.

- Add some name to the new folder and it will become part of my drive folders just like the previous ones.

Google Docs

Google Docs can be thought of as the online version of PowerPoint, Microsoft Word, and Excel. In the language of Google Docs, you will call them Presentation, Google Document, and Spreadsheet respectively.

Once the registration process is completed the user is then directed to the following page of Google Drive.

As indicated in the picture, the Google Drive panel is further divided into three major parts.

• Towards the left, you can see the folder view which contains all those files which are present as shared files, modified files as well as the files starred by the user

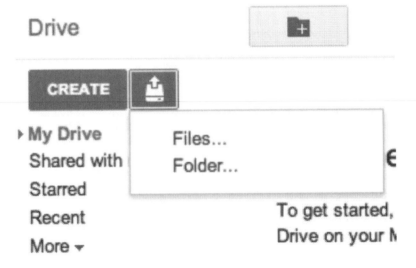

• Over the top lies the menu bar which carries all the options including the creation of new folders, sorting of files, various viewing and setting option.

- The center area of the drive is the one which carries all files available in the Drive. These files will all be displayed in this center portion. Initially, when the user will just start with the drive and there will be no files in his or her drive then this central part will be occupied with the information regarding Google Drive.

- **Adding files in your Google Drive:**

Two different methods can be applied to create files for your Google drive.

- The first method relates to the creation of an empty file from the very beginning. It is accomplished by clicking on the button named "Create".

- The second method entails an uploading of the existing file over the Drive and working with it afterward. For this method, you will click the Hard disk icon having arrow button as well as the choose file icon and create button

You will come across an upload file panel. Now browse for the specific file which you intend to upload to the Google Drive. Click on the specific file and select upload. When this process will be completed, you will get the specific panel which is shown below:

Now when you will close the panel for the file upload, the Google drive will show that particular file in the drive.

The picture below depicts the same procedure in which the file which we uploaded in previous steps can be seen in the central part of the drive, which is fixed for the files available in the Drive.

Converting the non-native (uploaded) documents to Google Docs:

You can see in the previous steps that the file which was uploaded to the Google Drive was having the icon "W" with it.

It indicates that although it is residing in your Google Drive, yet it is still in the Microsoft Document form and is not in the Google Doc form.

In this part of the book, we will deal with conversion of a document to Google Doc form, which is necessary to make modifications and editing in the document.

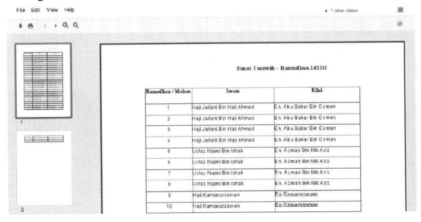

You can see it if you click on the file which you have uploaded to the drive. Opening a document in the original form will not let you make any changes in the document. For making it editable and compatible with the Google Drive you need to make a Google Doc version of it.

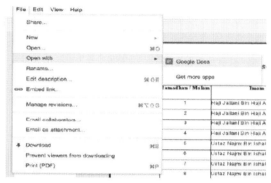

Click on "File" then "Open With" and then select "Google Docs".

After this step, the original file uploaded in the Word format will appear as Google Docs. You can then open this file in a separate editor.

Any kind of modifications and editing can quickly be done now on this Google Doc file. Now if you just close the editor tab and go to the home page of Google Drive you can easily see that there will be two separate files in the field area.

One will be the original version of the file which was uploaded in the first step. The second will be the one which you just converted into the Google Doc format.

In this case, one thing which is essential to remember is that the modifications will be stored in the Google Doc file so if you want to use the changed and modified file you will need to click the Google Doc version.

The word format file will reside as it was in the original format at the time of uploading. This should be dealt with care while considering official and corporate matters.

TIPS AND TRICKS FOR THE TEACHER

Learn All the Ways to Give Feedback.

Your students will thrive with as much feedback as you can provide them, and Classroom offers you many options for this. You can leave comments on assignments that students' hand in, on the file submitted, through email, and so much more. Consider the best places to leave feedback and let your students know to be on the lookout for ways to improve.

Some of the ways that you can utilize comments include:

Class comments—you can do this by starting a common for the whole class outside the assignment or in the announcement. This will be a comment that the entire course is going to see, so don't use it if you want to talk to the individual student. It is an excellent option to use if you're going to answer a question that many people have.

Private comments—you can do this by going into the file of an individual student. You will see the submissions this student has made and can click on the comment bar near the bottom. When you add a comment, the student will be the only one who can see it.

Comments to media—you can do this by clicking on the file that the student submitted to you. Highlight the area and then comment on that particular part of the project. This can help you show an example of the student or explain your thoughts and how something needs to be changed.

Use the Description Feature

When creating an assignment, make sure to add a nice long description. This is where you explain what the task is all about; complete it, and even when the job is due. Often students are juggling many classes all at once, and by the time they get to the task, they have forgotten all the instructions you gave them in class. Or if a student missed class that day, the description can help them understand what they missed. A good story can help limit emails with questions and help students get started on the assignment without confusion.

Use Flubaroo

Grading can take up a lot of your time, especially when dealing with many students and multiple classes. You want to provide your students with accurate feedback as quickly as possible, but traditional teaching can make this impossible. Add-ons like Flubaroo can make this easier. When creating a quiz or test, you can use Flubaroo so that when a student submits their answers, the app will check them and provide a score right away. The student can see how well they did on the quiz and where they may need to make some changes.

This kind of add-on is best for things such as multiple-choice assignments and tests. It allows the student to see what they understand right away without waiting for the teacher to correct everything. You can go back and change the grade on a particular assignment if the add-on grades incorrectly, add bonus points, or some other reason.

If you are creating assignments like discussion posts, opinions, projects, and essays, Flubaroo is not the best option. This app will not understand how to grade these projects, and since each one is more creative and doesn't necessarily have a right or wrong answer, the teacher needs to go in and rank. There are many places where you can provide feedback, even at various points of the project, to help the student make changes before the final grade.

Reuse Some of Your Old Posts

At times, you may have an assignment, question, or announcement that is similar to something you have posted before. For example, if you have a weekly reading or discussion assignment that is pretty much the same every week, you will use the reuse option in the Classroom. Just click on the "+" button that is on the bottom right of the screen. You will then be able to select "Reuse post." Pick from a list of options that you already used for the class. If there are any modifications, such as a different due date, you can make those before posting again. When reusing the post, you have the option to create new copies of the attachments that were used in the original posting.

Share Your Links and Resources

There may be times that you find a fascinating document, video, or other media that you would like your students to see. Or they may need resources for an upcoming project, and you want to make it easier for them to find. In this case, you should use the announcement feature. This allows all the essential documents to be listed right at the Classroom's top rather than potentially getting lost further down in assignments.

273

This is a great tip to use for items of interest that you would like to share with your students or documents and files that they will need right away. If you have a resource that the students will need throughout the year, you should place it into the "About" tab to prevent it from getting lost as the year goes on.

CONCLUSION

With Google Classroom many teachers have taken the first step to changing how they run their classroom. It's a platform that can be used to help teachers and students alike benefit from this activity. With Google Classroom, you get the extra benefit of being able to help plan your classrooms effectively, and get students into the spirit of taking their education to new heights. Teachers love this system because it keeps everything in one place. The advent of virtual classrooms and having everything on the computer, has only made learning more accessible.

Google is coming out with new and improved learning tools as well, such as the tablets that you can get for your students, which help them keep learning. With these additions, along with Google Classroom, your ability to teach the students core curriculum that they need to be successful is possible and worth it.

With that being said, let's discuss the next step that you as an educator, parent, guardian or student should take to get the most out of this. For teachers, start to plan your lessons based off this system, and put together the plan and such. You can from there, with the parents and students, get into this, and you can all keep up with the child's education. Many parents have trouble taking the initiative, but if you have it all together, you'll be able to create the perfect scholarly plan for your pupils. Everyone can learn what

they want to learn with this amazing system. Learning is being taken to a new, digital future and Google Classroom is providing that, and so much more.

Google Classroom does not allow access to multi-domain. Event feed doesn't change automatically, so learners need to review and refresh to avoid missing essential announcements periodically. Thus, Google Classroom comes with both benefits and drawbacks.

Nevertheless, the benefits far outweigh the cons. Instructors may fill in subtopics and apply tags to classwork, using emoji or text abbreviations, to find a suitable structure for a well-organized Google class. Reviews and feedbacks are critical for bringing in new functionality to the Classroom at Google platform. Teachers can use announcements to provide the students with essential links, docs/files, and videos they'll need immediately. Teachers don't need to answer every question! They should give the students the power of mutual support. Use the icon "+" to construct a query for a given task or project. It will serve as a discussion forum where students will encourage each other. Having the learning goals attached to each task or activity in Google's Classroom will keep reminding the students what each learning activity aims to be. With a few tips and strategies, Google Classroom could be made productive, efficient, and even more useful.

Google Classroom has every chance of becoming a popular international online learning platform (some functions are currently in beta testing). Nowadays, when virtually all types of content are moving from analog, physical and static to digital, this is a great chance to make the education system as flexible and personalized as possible

Printed in Great Britain
by Amazon

56369051R00160